Books by Richard B. Lyttle

PEOPLE OF THE DAWN
Early Man in the Americas

WAVES ACROSS THE PAST
Adventures in Underwater Archaeology

THE GAMES THEY PLAYED
Sports in History

THE GOLDEN PATH
The Lure of Gold Through History

Land
Beyond
the River

RICHARD B. LYTTLE

Land Beyond the River

Europe in the Age of Migration

WITH ILLUSTRATIONS BY THE AUTHOR

Atheneum 1986 New York

Library of Congress Cataloging-in-Publication Data

Lyttle, Richard B.   Land beyond the river.

Bibliography: p. 166.
Includes index.
SUMMARY: Describes how the migrating Huns,
barbarians, Moslems, Vikings, Mongols, and others changed
the face of Europe between the 2nd and 9th centuries.
1. Migrations of nations—Juvenile literature.
2. Europe—History—392-814—Juvenile literature.
[1. Migrations of nations. 2. Europe—History—392-814]
I. Title.
D135.L97   1986   940.1   85-28758
ISBN 0-689-31199-0

Published simultaneously in Canada by
Collier Macmillan Canada, Ltd.
Composition by Maryland Linotype, Baltimore, Maryland
Printed and bound by Fairfield Graphics, Fairfield, Pennsylvania
Designed by Mary Ahern
First Edition

This book is for my editor,
MARCIA MARSHALL

CONTENTS

The Roman Empire at the beginning of the Age of Migration.

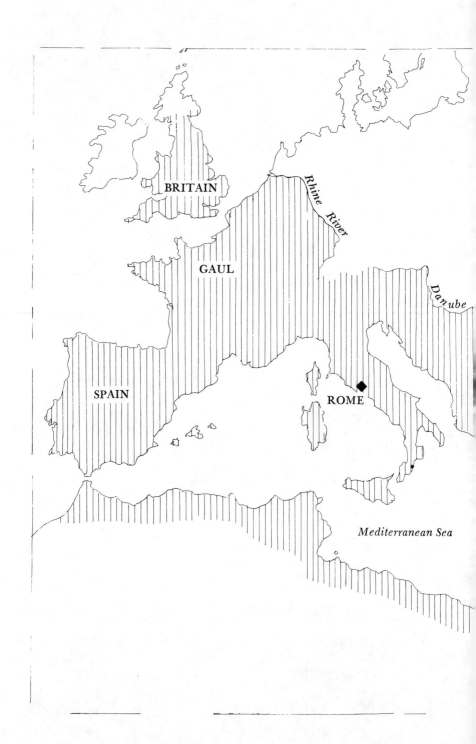

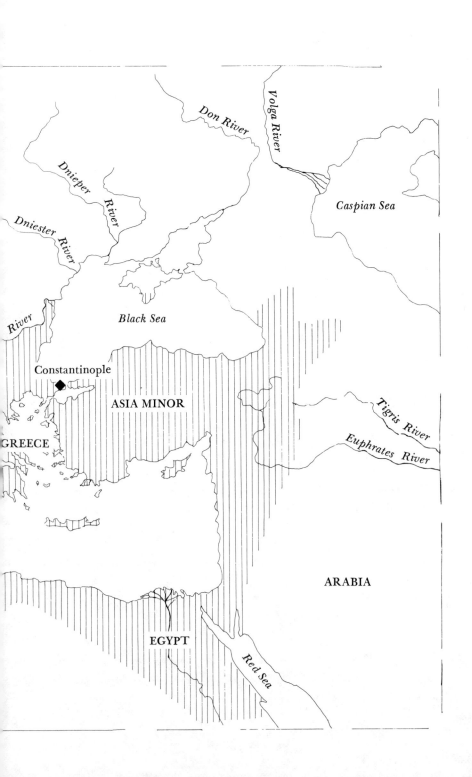

Land
Beyond
the River

Fort Ross, preserved as an historical monument, is a popular tourist attraction on the northern California coast.

Chapter One

The Restless Spirit

On a California slope overlooking the Pacific Ocean a stockade of hewn timbers surrounds a small church, an armory, and several other wooden buildings. Each corner of the stockade is protected by a sturdy blockhouse, and the walls of each blockhouse are punctuated by menacing gun ports.

Fort Ross, some sixty miles north of San Francisco, looks like a typical pioneer outpost of the American West.

But it is a different and unique landmark. The stockade and the cluster of old buildings were established by adventurers from the Old World. The small church holds icons and relics inspired by a faith rooted in far away Constantinople (now Istanbul, Turkey). The armory held weapons and gunpowder supplied by the tsar's government in Moscow. The other buildings housed Russian soldiers and fur traders. Fort Ross symbolizes a restless spirit and energy that goes far back in time.

Such restlessness did indeed contribute to the western expansion across our own continent, but this familiar story is recent history. There are earlier, not so familiar stories showing that the urge to migrate, to extend one's horizons, to explore the land beyond the river is an urge that seems to have been part of the human condition since civilization began. Indeed, the restless urge had shaped the boundaries of the Old World long before the New World was discovered.

Rome still ruled most of the known world when the Age of Migration began. Although it was centered on the Mediterranean Sea, the empire stretched from Britain to the west all the way to Mesopotamia and the Arabian Desert to the east. At its height, the Roman frontier was ten thousand miles long. This frontier was not heavily defended. The general policy was to rely on rivers and other natural barriers for defense, and only at the trouble spots had walls and forts been built. Thus, the frontier across Europe followed the Rhine River into the Alps, and beyond the Alps it followed the Danube River down to the Black Sea.

Although the Roman Empire was vast, its glory was fading. The government had wasted much patience and energy trying vainly to suppress Christianity. Meanwhile,

decadence, particularly among the ruling class, had under-
mined the creative drive that had built the empire. By
the third century, most emperors were more interested in
gaining and holding power than in using it fairly and to
good purpose. With few exceptions, they sought personal
gain and pleasure. And they were willing to kill for it.
Assassination became all too common.

During Rome's slow decline, very few emperors died
naturally. Assassination hardly encouraged good government. Emperors who took the throne by the knife could
hardly win full trust from the people, let alone put much
trust in those who served them. Another knife could be
easily hidden under an ambitious "friend's" toga.

Roman citizens, once the foundation of empire, lost
their pride in service and their faith in the leaders. In the
earlier days, when almost every citizen had served in the
army, the Empire had steadily expanded its borders. Rome
won rich colonies and conquered peoples were given
Roman law and Roman government, not to mention dur-
able Roman roads, bridges, aqueducts, and buildings.

As long as it was expanding, the empire prospered,
but prosperity softened the people. In time, citizens refused to serve in the army. Mercenaries had to be hired
to protect the borders. It became the policy to hire men
from the border territories. Thus non-Roman mercenaries
were hired to defend the borders against other non-
Romans who threatened to invade the empire. Despite
the obvious weakness of this policy, it worked for many
years. But the empire no longer expanded. Instead, its
borders gradually began to shrink.

The fabulous wealth that had built Rome and other
glittering cities began to diminish. Farmers who had once
thrived on small plots of land sold their land to cover

debts and moved into the cities to join a growing class of poor and undernourished people and so the productivity of the land diminished. Most goods, even grain and other necessities, had to be imported from distant provinces. The nobility continued to waste their wealth on jewels, spices, furs, and other luxuries, but eventually, even their money began to give out.

The empire itself faced bankruptcy. Desperately, emperors killed the leaders of some of the remaining rich families and confiscated their assets to keep the government running. Roman coinage, once the mainstay of world commerce, was devalued again and again until it became useless. The mercenary soldiers demanded gold. Often their demands could not be met. Border raids increased.

A few courageous emperors tried to restore Rome to its former glory and power. In 284 A.D., Diocletian, a reformer put in power by the army, decided that the borders could be better defended if the empire were divided. A new capital of government was created in Byzantium, soon to be called Constantinople, and now Istanbul.

In 313 A.D., Constantine I, who gave his name to the new city, ended long religious persecution by giving Christianity equal status with other faiths. He then went farther and divided the empire into Christian provinces and appointed bishops to administer them. Thus the church gained tremendous civil as well as religious power, but the unity of the empire itself was further diminished. Rome's political importance waned.

Meanwhile, the mass movement of barbarians, the Germanic tribes beyond the borders, began. Although often poor and sometimes homeless, they were not entirely uncivilized. True, the Latin *barbari*, when used by

*Constantine I gave Christianity equal
status with the other religions of Rome.*

the Romans, was intended as an insult. The word meant
uneducated and rough, but it did not fairly describe the
tribes. Through many generations of contact with Greeks
and Romans, most barbarians had learned to respect the
achievements of the empire, including art and literature.
Some barbarians could read and write.

Rather than destroy the empire, barbarians usually sought to preserve it so they could enjoy its stability and its bounty. But the tribes had high birth rates. New land was desperately needed to feed an ever-growing population. In many regions the best land lay within the empire. This land, often sparsely settled, waited beyond the rivers and other poorly defended borders.

Although individual barbarian families undoubtedly crossed the borders by the thousands, it was safer to move with the clan or tribe. Among the many Germanic tribes, the Burgundians, Angles, Saxons, Jutes, Alani, Thuringians, Franks, Quadi, Vandals, Ostrogoths, Visigoths, Seuvi, Frisians, Lombards, and Alemanni were the largest and best known.

Organization and strong leadership was needed to move armed men and their families into hostile lands. In the later migrations described in this book, the record tells of leaders with remarkable character and courage.

Islam was created by the amazing Mohammed. Under the tireless Genghis Khan, the Mongols almost conquered the entire known world. Personalities could even have a negative influence, for Siberia's wide rivers were crossed by pioneers wanting to escape from authority, including the authority of Ivan the Terrible, one of history's most fascinating despots.

Unfortunately, because of a slim and biased record, we know little about the leaders of the early migrations. During the fourth and fifth centuries, every Greek or Roman writer who could hold a pen damned the barbarians and their leaders. Even when barbarians wanted nothing more than the right to settle unused land, Romans feared them as uncouth invaders. It is true that barbarians could be cruel and bloodthirsty, but they also must have been courageous and daring. The record that has come down to us, however, rarely mentions any virtues.

Few writers of the day realized or would admit that the tribes were forced to migrate. If they were to survive the population pressures of their own and neighboring tribes, they had no other choice.

The pressures worked by chain reaction. When one tribe moved, it put pressure on another, forcing it to move and, in turn, pressuring yet another tribe. The greatest of these chain reactions was started not by barbarians, but by the Huns who traced their origin back to the Far East.

Although we don't know exactly what made the Huns cross the Volga River in the latter half of the fourth century, there was probably good cause. Perhaps they were being pressured by expanding populations to the east. Maybe a series of droughts had destroyed vital pasturage. We do know that the Huns set almost all of the barbarian world in motion.

The Huns' army failed to reach Rome, but their attempt set an example for others. The Visigoths sacked the ancient city in 410 A.D., the Vandals came in 450 A.D. By then, however, Rome had lost its political importance. In fact, the western capital had already been shifted to Ravenna on the Adriatic Coast before the invaders came.

But Rome remained as the symbol of past power and wealth. And thanks to some stubborn churchmen, it became the religious center of the West. Despite all perils of siege and invasion, the bishops of Rome would not abandon the city. This proved to be significant. As time passed, the office of bishop gained more and more influence and respect, far more than intended when Constantine I divided his realm into church provinces.

The original idea was that the bishop or patriarch of

Constantinople would head all Christendom. This plan worked for a time, but Constantinople was far from Rome. Sometimes it was isolated by barbarians, making it impossible for the western faithful to receive guidance from Constantinople. Gradually the bishop of Rome, soon to be called "Father" or "Pope," built a sphere of influence that spread far beyond the walls of the old city.

The popes established an early tradition of independence. They often defied the orders of the barbarian kings and chieftains who were trying to dominate the West. And the popes sometimes ignored or even refused to obey orders from faraway Constantinople.

While the patriarchs in Constantinople were appointed by the emperors and gave their support to the government, the popes established their own system for succession, which gave them independence from civil authority.

The independence of Rome became an important difference between eastern and western church administration and philosophy. Another important difference was language. Priests of the eastern church conducted religious services in Greek. Priests of the western church conducted services in Latin. There were additional, minor differences. Eastern priests, who always wore beards, were allowed to marry. Marriage was to be denied priests in the West.

Through the years, there were several efforts to unite East and West. The leaders of both churches met in conferences of unity. Debate sometimes lasted for months. But no workable agreements could be made. In some cases the conferences only served to emphasize the differences, particularly the language difference, that separated East

and West. So the Roman Catholic Church and the Orthodox Eastern Church remain separate to this day.

Meanwhile, Constantinople gained the political and
economic strength to govern an empire that embraced all
the eastern territories of the old Roman world. The
Byzantine Empire, as it became known, was to last more
than one thousand years. It nurtured a remarkably stable
civilization, and its influence spread far beyond its borders,
and wherever its influence reached, it carried with it the
Orthodox faith.

Thanks to Byzantine influence, Russia adopted the
Orthodox Eastern Church. Thus when hardy Russians
extended their fur trading domain into California, they
built an Orthodox church in their small, remote stockade.

Chapter Two

The Huns

They killed children without mercy. They violated young girls and nuns. They drank human blood. They cut the cheeks of their own babies to harden them against pain. And they were ugly.

These terrifying accounts were encouraged by the Huns themselves. They wanted to be feared. It was part of their strategy of conquest. They knew that a frightened enemy was half-beaten before a battle began.

The superb horsemen of Asia—the Hsuing-nu as they were called in China—thrived on battle. And they usually won. They came from the cold plains near China where the Mongolian Republic is today. For many generations, the fierce warriors raided Chinese cities. In some years the Chinese paid tribute to the Huns to soften their craving for plunder. But the Huns needed land as well as treasure. For many years some of their bands occupied Northern China and grazed their herds there.

In the third century B.C. the Chinese began building a stone barrier along their border. The Great Wall, as it

This bronze casting of a mounted horseman found in Northwestern China probably depicts a Hsuing-Nu or Hun warrior. Certainly, the short, hook-nosed horse with a bushy tail fits later descriptions of Hun steeds.

became known, did not stop the raids entirely, but it did force many Huns to seek booty elsewhere. Most of the hordes turned west, to begin a migration that would take them to the heart of Europe.

They moved slowly. It was not until about 355 A.D. that the Huns entered southern Russia. There, they forced most of the Sarmatians, the native nomads of the region, into the Balkans. The Sarmatians in turn pressured the Goths who retreated to the borders of the Roman Empire. Thus began a restless time of fear, hunger, and bloodshed, a time we now call the Age of Migration.

Of all the migratory tribes of history, the Huns did more than any others in shaping the map of Europe. By upsetting the balance of power along the frontiers, they hastened the fall of Rome.

Rome was first sacked by an army composed largely of Hun mercenaries. They changed the nature of warfare. For one thousand years after their first appearance in Europe, battles would not be dominated by foot soldiers as in the past, but by warriors mounted on swift horses. The Huns' cruel and destructive ways set back the civilizing influences of religion and culture by many centuries.

Although the Huns vanished as an organized force after barely one hundred years in Europe, they had set a pattern for other eastern nomads. The Mongols, as we shall see, followed eight centuries later to play a bloody role that also shaped the destiny of Europe.

Ironically, as influential as the Huns were, we know very little about them. Illiterate, they left no written record of their own. The surviving accounts about them were all written by their enemies. Thus, most of the record is coated with bias.

Jordanes, the sixth century historian, credited the Huns' conquest to their ugliness.

"By the terror of their features they inspire great fear in those whom they did not really surpass in war. They made their foes flee in horror because their swarthy aspect was fearful, and they had . . . a shapeless lump instead of a head, with pinholes rather than eyes. They are cruel to their children on the very day of their birth. For they cut the cheeks of the males with a sword, so that before they receive the nourishment of milk, they must learn to endure wounds. Hence they grow old beardless with faces scarred by the sword."

But Jordanes did have some grudging praise:

"They are short in stature, quick in body movement, alert horsemen, ready in the use of bow and arrow, broad shouldered, and with firm set necks always erect in pride."

*Although Roman writers claimed that all Huns were ugly,
these death masks, formed in a sheet of thin gold and placed in
a Hun grave, suggest some noble features.*

Obviously, being Asiatics, the Huns did look different
to the Europeans. They also had different beliefs.

Although many Europeans still worshipped the old
Roman and Greek gods, there was a new faith—Chris-
tianity. It was gaining thousands of enthusiastic followers.
Soon both Rome in the West and Constantinople in the
East would be vying for leadership as defenders of the new
faith.

The Huns worshipped deities of nature and believed
in the power of shamans, which were something like witch
doctors. Shamans could cure the sick, read omens, interpret dreams, and see into the future. Each tribe of Huns
looked to at least one person who was believed to have
shaman power.

Before deciding to cross a river, go into battle, or
take any other major step, Huns consulted their shamans.
Often on such occasions, the shaman would throw the
shoulder blades of a freshly killed animal into a fire. When

the flesh had been burned away, the shoulder blades were taken from the ashes and the lines and cracks on the bones were "read" to tell if a planned venture would be a success.

Although looks and religious belief set the Huns apart, these differences did not alone make them a threat. It was an economic difference that made the Huns so dangerous.

While most Europeans had given up hunting and large-scale animal herding to become farmers, the Huns depended on huge herds of sheep, cattle, and horses. A European farm family had learned to survive with a few acres of plowed land. The Huns needed vast pastures, and so it was necessary for them to keep moving in search of fresh pastures.

As the Huns moved westward, they encountered more and more plowed land. Such land could become useful to the Huns only after the farmers were driven off and the plowing stopped. Thus if the Hun conquest was to succeed, it had to be harsh. Farmers who did not flee before the hordes were killed or sold into slavery in order to clear the land.

The fear the Huns generated made it possible for small raiding parties, working independently, to gain vast territories without major battles. These Hun raids were swift and unpredictable. They made it seem the Huns had no king or leader, and to have no home base. A proverb of the day said: "A Hun's country is the back of his horse."

We know that Huns carried their kitchens with them in the form of large cauldrons designed with broad-based pedestals. These could be strapped on a horse's back just behind the rider. The cauldrons could carry hot coals for

Cauldrons like this bronze specimen found in southern Russia were strapped upright to a horse's rump right behind the rider, allowing Huns to carry warm food or even hot coals to the next camp.

the next campfire or food cooking from the heat of hot stones. The designs on some of these iron vessels give us some of the best surviving examples of primitive Hun art.

The Huns rode hooked-nosed, bushy-tailed horses which were so small that the rider's feet barely cleared the ground. The steeds were agile enough and strong enough, however, to serve extremely well in battle. With lightning speed, the Hun horsemen could scatter and regroup so quickly that their victims often did not know where to run.

Much of the credit for the Hun success in conquest must go to these sturdy horses. While the pampered Roman horse would sicken after a night in the rain, the Hun horse could fend for itself in winter pasture and be ready for hard work the moment it was needed. And small as it was, the Hun horse carried a saddle and a variety of weapons as well as an armored warrior.

Hun saddles were made of felt or leather, reinforced with wood, but there apparently were no stirrups—which

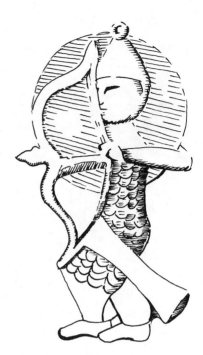

*A bronze pendant
found in a Hun grave shows
the unbalanced bow,
hour-glass quiver, and scale
armor that were typical
Hun equipment.*

makes the Hun marksmanship with bow and arrow all the more remarkable. Without stirrups to brace the feet, it would be difficult to handle any weapon. The Huns, however, used lances, swords, and lassoes as well as bows and arrows.

They were superb archers. They used a short, composite war bow. It was strengthened with strips of bone or sinew glued to the back and sides. When fully drawn, the bow could send an arrow fifty-five to sixty-five yards with deadly accuracy. Actually, most Hun warriors could hit targets one hundred seventy-five to one hundred eighty-five yards away.

Unfortunately for the record both armor and bows were apparently too valuable to be buried with a warrior. Archeologists explain the lack of finds by speculating that bows and armor were passed down to sons or other relatives. The few bow fragments that have been found show remarkable craftsmanship. Certainly, highly trained experts were needed, craftsmen who devoted their life to the bow-making art. The Hun bow apparently was not symmetrical, the top arm being longer than the bottom arm. This meant that the bowmaker had to reinforce the arms with different thicknesses of bone or sinew to make sure that the bow pulled with equal balance and fired truly.

Modern craftsmen who have tried to copy the ancient art have concluded that it might take no more than four or five days to make a bow, but adjustments to "tune" a bow to perfection might require many months. No wonder Hun warriors did not allow good bows to be buried with the dead! Besides, the shamans said that the dead were beyond harm. They needed no weapons to protect themselves.

Hun warriors also carried small shields and usually wore leather helmets and armor. Some nomads of the time made a scale armor out of the bony hooves of horses. The hooves were sliced and dried to produce thin but hard half-disks. Overlapping rows of these disks were then sewn onto leather vests or jackets to make a light, protective armor. Hun men may have worn such armor, but some accounts say that they had bronze or iron breastplates and helmets. Such helmets were reportedly fitted with a front plate just wide enough to protect the nose. It's possible, however, that only the higher class Huns—the nobility— had the advantage of metal armor and helmets.

Huns apparently used their lances for thrusting rather than throwing. With the point of the lance lowered and the butt braced against the saddle, a charging horseman could terrorize the bravest foot soldier. A line of charging lancers would have little trouble scattering a defensive formation, particularly if it had already been "softened" by a torrent of arrows.

In close combat with other horsemen, Hun warriors would catch enemy riders in lasso nooses and pull them from their saddles. Swords were also used with deadly effect against both foot soldiers and mounted warriors. Again, little archeological evidence has been gathered, but we can assume that the Hun sword differed little from the short but handy Roman sword of the day.

Hun shields were small and light, usually made by stretching leather over a round framework made of wood, but it can be assumed that when the Huns or their allies fought on foot, as was sometimes necessary in rough terrain, they carried a larger shield. One account tells of Hun soldiers leaning on their shields during a parley. This suggests an oblong shield long enough to protect both body and legs.

In southern Russia the Huns allied themselves with a group of Sarmatians, another nomad tribe of the Steppes who were known as the Alans, and in about 372 A.D. the combined army crossed the Volga River into the Ukraine, home of the Ostrogoths, one of the more civilized Germanic peoples.

Ermanaric, the one hundred-year-old Ostrogoth king, led his men into desperate battle. He fought bravely, but he was killed, and his army was defeated. Some survivors surrendered and joined the Huns. Others fled westward to the region north of the Danube then occupied by the other Goth tribe, the Visigoths. The Huns followed.

The Visigoths, overwhelmed by an advance army of Hun cavalry, fled across the Danube River where, as we shall see, another bloody saga began.

Meanwhile, the Huns did a strange thing. They settled down. Apparently the rich land and its produce impressed the nomadic Huns so much that they began to

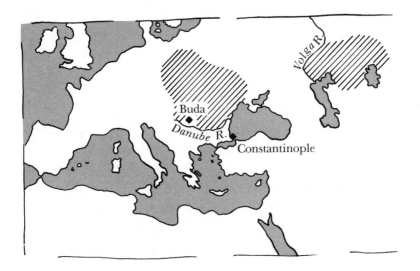

The Huns remained east of the Volga until late in the fourth century. In about 372 A.D., they crossed the great river in force, began dislocating native tribes, and touched off a chain reaction of migrations. The Huns eventually settled north of the Danube, and from their capital at Buda, they continued to send shock waves of influence and pressure throughout Europe.

see the benefits of a farming economy. Few were actually farmers. But many became farm owners, content to let slaves work the land for them. The Huns brought more and more Germanic tribes under their rule until they dominated what is now known as the Plain of Hungary, north of the Danube River.

For a time, it seems, various Hun clans acted independently. Many warriors joined the battle across the Danube to the south, some fighting with the Visigoths and others fighting against them. Hun cavalry units were also hired in the west by Roman generals. And in their own territory, Huns sometimes fought among themselves.

Strong leadership was needed to unite such people. Historians of the time spoke of Hun kings, but they were more likely chieftans, commanding no more than a few clans. King Rua, however, was apparently more than a chief. He commanded many clans, and he may have been the first to demand and get tribute from both Rome and Constantinople. For an annual treasure of gold, Rua agreed to leave the frontiers in peace. This extortion continued long after Rua died.

Although exact dates in most Hun histories are suspect, King Rua, by all accounts, died in 433 A.D. His kingdom went to two nephews, Bleda and Attila. They ruled jointly until about 444 when Bleda was slain, probably by Attila.

There can be no doubt that Attila, which is a Gothic name meaning "little father," was the most powerful Hun leader we know of. He was to expand the Hun empire from the River Don on the east and all the way to the Rhine River on the west.

Of him Jordanes wrote:

"He was a man born into the world to shake the nations, the scourge of all lands, who in some way terrified all mankind by the rumors noised abroad concerning him. He was haughty in his walk, rolling his eyes hither and thither, so that the power of his proud spirit appeared in the movement of his body. He was indeed a lover of war, yet restrained in action; mighty in counsel, gracious to suppliants, and lenient to those who were once received under his protection. He was short of stature, with a broad chest and a large head; his eyes were small, his beard was thin and sprinkled with gray. He had a flat nose and a swarthy complexion, revealing his origin."

Attila probably showed more restraint to his enemies than most previous Hun rulers, but he was master of the scare story, believing that fear was one of the best weapons the Huns had. In the Christian world he soon became known as "the Scourge of God."

The title probably amused Attila. In his capital vil-

lage, at the site of present-day Buda, he built a palace of
logs. The walls and floors of this large, one-story building
were carefully planed and polished. It was decorated with
animal skins, carpets, and wooden carvings.

Unlike some of the Hun nobles of his court, Attila
dressed simply and was moderate in his eating and drinking habits. He did not wear a gold-studded sword belt, or
use gold harness when he rode in battle. He wore plain
rather than embroidered tunics.

*This Hun diadem set with semi-precious stones may have
graced the head of some noble lady in Attila's court.*

Although he could not read or write, Attila invited
travelers and scholars to his court in order to learn as
much as he could about the world. The "Scourge of God"
was not a savage, but he did see himself as ruler of every
corner of the world that his scholars described to him.

And why not? He could put a half-million horsemen
in the field. No other force could stand against them.
Theodosius II, ruler of the Eastern Empire, and Emperor Valentinian, who ruled the West, each paid Attila

seven hundred pounds of gold annually. The tribute was an admission of weakness.

Perhaps Attila was thinking of gold when he sent his army across the Danube. The Hun forces quickly captured four cities and were getting ready to attack Constantinople itself when Theodosius II sent an army against them. When the Huns defeated the imperial army, Constantinople asked for peace. Attila said he would call back his horsemen only if Theodosius raised the tribute from seven hundred to two thousand one hundred pounds of gold a year. The emperor agreed.

The Hun army withdrew, but they did not keep their side of the bargain for long. In about 447, the army crossed the Danube again and sacked some seventy towns, killing and taking slaves wherever they went. Women were forced to join Hun harems, beginning the mixture of blood that would leave Mongol traits as far west as Germany.

Meanwhile, Attilla threw the Balkan provinces into such chaos that four centuries would pass before prosperity returned. And the Danube River itself ceased to be an avenue of commerce and communication between the Eastern and Western Empires. Barges were no longer seen on the big river. Towns along the river banks were abandoned. In effect, the Hun tribes had driven a wedge between the two parts of the Roman Empire. Culturally and politically, East and West henceforth would develop separately.

Attila was eyeing the weakening of the West closely. All he needed was an excuse to attack. The excuse was provided by a woman of the Roman court, a romantic and perhaps foolish woman.

Honoria, sister of Valentinian III, the new emperor

in Rome, had been sent to Constantinople in shame. She had earned this banishment by allowing herself to be seduced by one of Valentinian's chamberlains.

There was undoubtedly more to this romantic tale than the historians have recorded, but we do know that Honoria was very eager to escape from her banishment in Constantinople. Thinking Attila might rescue her, she sent him a ring and a plea for help. Attila interpreted Honoria's message as an offer of marriage and answered that he would gladly be her husband. This was not exactly what Honoria had in mind, but it fit Attila's purposes perfectly. We can also guess that it tickled his sense of humor.

Without wasting any time, he ordered his ambassadors in Rome to ask for half the Western Empire as the bride's dowry. Just as Attila expected, Valentinian III refused. The Huns attacked.

In about 451, Attila led an army of half a million across the Rhine into northeastern Gaul (France). His forces sacked Trier, killing all the inhabitants. Metz next fell to the same fate. The Huns continued toward the heart of Gaul. They planned to destroy every town and city in their path until they reached Rome.

The Roman army was led by Aetius, an experienced and courageous general. He knew that the Roman legions alone could not challenge the Huns and looked desperately for help. Fortunately the Visigoths, a tribe almost destroyed by earlier encounters with the Huns, had migrated as far as southern Gaul. These Germanic people, led by the aging Theodoric I, had good reason to want to avenge themselves. And now they stood in the path of the advancing horde.

Theodoric I joined forces with Aetius and his legions.

The allied army met the Huns on the Catalaunian Fields near Troyes some ninety miles east of Paris. It was one of history's bloodiest battles. Reports have it that one hundred sixty-two thousand men died. It's hard to say which side won.

Attila was turned back, but he retreated in good order. Within a year his army would attack again. The Romans and the Visigoths were either too exhausted or not well enough organized to pursue the retreating Huns. Theodoric, who might have led a force after them, had been killed in the battle.

The following year, Attila attacked Italy as planned. One town in northeastern Italy was destroyed so completely it never rose again. Vicenza and Verona next fell to the Hun hordes. Pavia and Milan surrendered all moveable wealth to keep them out.

Here, in Italy, there were no Visigoths to help, and Aetius lacked the force to stop the Huns. But for some reason Attila delayed crossing the Po. Valentinian sent two Roman senators and Pope Leo I to sue for peace.

Some historians credit Leo for saving Rome. We don't know what was said at the peace conference, but soon after it ended, Attila led his army out of Italy. He may have been greatly influenced by the Pope, but there were other reasons for retreat. The troops were running short of food, and many among them were ill, perhaps with a kind of plague.

Attila, just the same, threatened to return to Italy the following spring if Honoria were not sent to him as his bride. Meanwhile, he was about to add a young girl named Ildico to his harem.

The wedding was celebrated in Attila's log palace. Although usually temperate, Attila ate and drank more than usual. He never saw another dawn. During the night, a blood vessel burst in his nose. The blood filled his lungs and suffocated him. Thus the most feared man of his day died of a nosebleed.

Attila's death in 453 marked the end of the Huns as a military force. His sons lacked the leadership to hold the realm together and within a few generations the Huns were assimilated into their former subjects. But they left a mark on history that has never been forgotten.

Chapter Three

God and
the Barbarians

The Age of Migration was a time of religious turmoil as well. The pagan gods were being replaced by a single, all-powerful god. It was a painful change, and paganism was slow to die. There were Romans and Greeks who continued to worship the old gods long after Christian emperors had declared paganism an offense punishable by death.

Adding to the turmoil was dissension within the new faith itself. Slight disagreements in belief caused riots and bloodshed among the Christians. The violence over "heresies" within the early Christian church was said to have left many more dead than the Romans did during the Christian persecutions.

Sometimes people were so divided by religious difference that they could not govern themselves sensibly or defend themselves effectively. The religious turmoil contributed to the weakness of the Roman Empire. But the turmoil was not limited to the empire. The barbarians were also affected. They too were abandoning old gods for the new faith.

The conversion began late in the third century, almost a century before the Huns crossed the Volga. A band of Goths, seeking slaves and treasure, raided Roman territory in Asia Minor. The Goths returned to their homeland north of the Danube River with many captives, including some Christians. From these Christian slaves and their descendants the Goths and other Germanic tribes acquired the new faith.

These so-called barbarians were intensely interested in religion, for long contact with Greeks and Romans had taught them the advantages of all aspects of "civilization." Although the Romans continued to call them *barbari*, or "letterless churls," many were teaching themselves to read and write. Most tribes had adopted a code of laws, and most followed higher moral standards than those followed, or simply ignored, by the citizens of the declining empire.

Many barbarians were noted for their courage, honesty, and hospitality. Although they often lacked the fine manners of Rome, they were willing to learn them. The Germanic Goths particularly were eager to participate in the civilized life of the empire. They respected Rome. They did not seek to destroy it.

Early Germanic tribes had worshipped almost as many gods as the early Greeks and the Romans. The German gods, however, were perhaps harsher, more austere. The hammer-wielding Thor was god of thunder, rain, and farming. Odin, or Wotan, ruled over wisdom, poetry, and war.

At first, as this scene from a stone monument suggests, the well-armed Romans found it easy to kill and collect the heads of the poorly-equipped barbarians. Later, however, after the barbarians adopted Roman armor and tactics, they became feared for their courage and skill and despised for their faith.

It is not hard to understand why many might be tempted to give up hard-hearted deities in favor of one, gentle, all-forgiving god and the zeal of the missionaries aided conversion immensely. Ulfilas, born in about 311 A.D. to captives taken by the Goths in the Asia Minor raid, was one of the first and most successful of these missionaries.

By an unhappy accident of history, Ulfilas taught the
Arian creed. At the time it was the creed in fashion.
Constantinius II, sitting on the throne in Constantinople,
was himself an Arian. And when the pagan Goths began
persecuting the newly converted Christian Goths, Constantinius gave Ulfilas and his small band protection south
of the Danube. Arianism, however, was later to be branded
heresy by bishops of Rome and Constantinople.

What was Arianism? The Bishop Arius (280?–336),
who gave the creed its name, believed that Christ was like
God but not the same as God. This countered orthodox
belief that Christ and God were equally divine.

In his missionary work Ulfilas apparently did not
waste breath arguing about such fine points. He had more
important tasks. His major undertaking, translating the
Bible from Greek into Gothic, was a triumph of scholarship. Until his day, Gothic had never been a written language. Ulfilas thus had to invent a Gothic alphabet in
order to create his Gothic Bible.

Cited today as the first appearance of German as a
written language, the work was complete except for one
chapter of the Old Testament. Ulfilas purposely omitted
the Book of Kings because he feared it would make war
seem attractive to the tribes that he was trying to pacify.

"Father our Thou in Heaven . . ."

*Ulfilas had to invent a new alphabet in order to translate the
Bible from Greek into written Gothic. Here are the first five
words of the Lord's Prayer.*

When Ulfilas ventured north of the Danube again, his virtue, his wisdom, and his reputation as a scholar went before him. He won thousands of converts among the Goths who in turn would carry on the missionary work among other barbarians in coming generations. All became Arians.

Arianism was just one of many heresies to trouble the early church. In Africa, the Donatists had split the faith. Donatists held that no sacrament administered by a priest in a state of sin had validity. The orthodox bishops opposed this creed on practical grounds. Who, after all, was without sin?

In the Near East the dispute was to center on Mary's divinity. Nestorius, an eloquent bishop in Constantinople, preached that Mary was the mother of the human nature, not the divine nature in Christ. This countered the orthodox view that saw Mary as the mother of both natures and therefore "the Mother of God."

Although Nestorious was exiled, he carried a great following with him. The creed survived his death, and Nestorian Christians eventually established colonies in Syria and other regions of the Middle East where they continued to trouble the Orthodox church.

The Orthodox bishops were intolerant of all heresies because they believed any argument over faith would undermine unity and thus destroy the church. If Christianity were to survive, the orthodox bishops held, it would be as "one faith." Indeed, there can be no doubt that the heresies, particularly Arianism, caused long-lasting intolerance, hate, and bloodshed.

To the Christians of the time the degree of Christ's divinity was a matter of life and death. There were riots. Churches that taught the Arian creed were burned to the ground, and in retaliation, Orthodox churches were destroyed. In one riot, three thousand Christians died.

Athanasius, the bishop of Alexandria in Egypt, was Arius's strongest, most vocal opponent. Both men gathered their own loyal followers, splitting the church in two.

The Council of Nicaea, called in 325 A.D., was supposed to resolve the question, but it did not. In ruling Arianism a heresy, the council only intensified the debate. Arius was first banished from Constantinople and then reinstated by the Emperor Constantine. Always trying to bring peace between the two factions, the emperor wrote to both Arius and Athanasius:

"The cause [of the debate] seems to be quite trifling, and unworthy of such fierce contests . . . There was no need to make these questions public . . . since they are problems which idleness alone raises, and whose only use is to sharpen men's wits . . . these are silly actions worthy of inexperienced children, and not of priests or reasonable men."

Constantine died in 337 without seeing the issue resolved. His Arian son, Constantinius II, rather than urge reconciliation, adopted Arianism as the state religion. It was he who gave shelter to Ulfilas and his converts. When Constantinius died, his successor, Julian, outraged all Christians by trying to restore the pagan faith. It was indeed an age of turmoil.

Arianism continued to spread among the barbarians. The Franks, who were to control most of Gaul, the Vandals, who were to invade North Africa, the Ostrogoths, who were to rule Italy for a generation, and the Visigoths, who were eventually to settle in Spain, all became Arian Christians. Orthodox Rome and Constantinople hated them for their heresy.

Although barbarians were often eager to accept Christianity, many retained part of their earlier faith. This coffin panel depicts a Christ that is crowned with the cross of the new faith and surrounded by animal forms of an old faith.

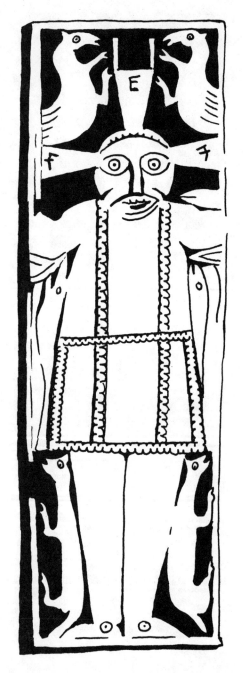

Surprisingly, the Orthodox cause would eventually be rescued by the Franks, one of the lustiest and least moral of all barbarian people. Through theft, cunning, stealth, and violence, the Franks had gradually expanded their realm from the Netherlands southward. They replaced or dominated the Romanized Gauls and eventually forced the Visigoths to retreat from Southern Gaul into Spain. They eventually changed the name of their realm from Gaul to Frank Land or France.

The Franks gave France a long-lasting reputation for brutality and bad manners. While most other barbarians had long honored the civilizing concepts of marriage, fidelity, and family responsibility, Frank chieftains continued to take several wives and concubines. But it so happened that in 481 A.D., Clovis, then just fifteen years old, was named king of the Franks. In the twelfth year of his reign, he married Clothilde, a Catholic or Orthodox Christian. Soon after, he and three thousand of his warriors were baptized in the same faith.

Thus began the conversion of all Franks, a conversion that laid the foundation for the Holy Roman Empire. For other barbarians, the Frankish conversion provided the example, and where necessary the Holy Roman Empire was to provide the force for conversions. Arianism gradually died out and Europe was united under one faith.

Chapter Four

The Goths

One of history's strangest ironies was provided by the Goths. They were among the first to come to terms with the Roman Empire. They were the most civilized of all the barbarian tribes. Many of them learned Latin or a crude form of the language. They adopted or at least respected Roman customs and laws, and when Christianity began to gain converts, the Goths, as we have seen, were among the first to accept the new faith.

Yet the Goths came to be the first "barbarians" to sack Rome.

Like other Germanic people, Goths had originated in Scandinavia. When they arrived in mainland Europe, most Goths apparently followed the Vistula River up to its source and then crossed over to the headwaters of the Dnieper River in Russia. By continuing on this southeastern track they eventually arrived at the northern shores of the Black Sea. There for some reason, the people divided.

One group, the Ostrogoths or eastern Goths, remained for many years in what is now the Ukraine Region of Russia. The other group, the Visigoths or western Goths, moved southwest to settle north of the Danube in a region that is now part of the Balkan States. There they came in close contact with the Romans.

It was usually good policy to cooperate with the empire. The Romans hired the German warriors as mercenaries to defend the frontiers. Often military service was rewarded with grants of land. This fit in with Rome's defensive policy, which encouraged peaceful barbarians to farm Roman territory. It not only made the land productive but also created a buffer against invasion by less

Eadwin, the British monk who wrote an illustrated description of life in medieval Europe, may have been depicting part-time soldiers who were called from their farms to repel invaders. It seems here that this Roman tradition was followed with considerable enthusiasm.

A seventh-century wall carving depicts a German warrior sitting somewhat awkwardly on his steed and suggesting that the man would be much more at ease fighting on foot. Foot soldiers, however, were fast being phased out when Gothic mercenaries enrolled in the Roman legions.

peaceful tribes. The warrior-farmers, wanting to save their land and crops, would be the first to fight the invaders.

The policy usually worked well. Even if the farmers were overrun, they delayed the invaders long enough for the legions to arrive and drive them out of the empire.

Many Goths admired the Roman talent for organization and the Roman craving for order and stability. And many Romans admired certain aspects of Goth culture. The Roman toga gradually gave way to the warmer, more practical barbarian trousers.

But more than anything, the Romans liked the fighting zeal of the barbarian warriors. When trained and disciplined in the Roman way of warfare, barbarian troops could stand against any armies in the known world. Indeed, the barbarians were taken into the Roman army in such numbers that by the middle of the fourth century, the legions were largely Germanic, often led by Germanic generals. One of these, the Vandal Stilicho, was, as we shall see, the most able military leader of his era. Again and again, he saved the empire from disaster.

Except when fighting Huns, the Germanic legions were called upon to repel Germanic invaders. Although the invaders usually outnumbered the defenders, the latter were better trained and equipped. The loosely organized invaders were usually repulsed, but they were rarely defeated. They regrouped and attacked again and again.

The reason for this was simple. The times were out of balance. The barbarian tribes all had higher birth rates than the Romans, but the Romans had a higher standard of living. This imbalance made invasion inevitable and almost continuous.

As long as they remained in the Ukraine, however, the Ostrogoths were not a threat to the empire. And they might have stayed in the Ukraine for all time if the Huns had not crossed the Volga. These Ostrogoths of the last half of the fourth century were apparently surprised by the invading Huns. They certainly were ill-prepared.

King Ermanaric, believed to be in his one hundredth year, led the Ostrogoths in a brave but hopeless defense. He was killed in the battle. His forces were overwhelmed. Some of the surviving warriors joined the enemy. The rest fled west with their families into the land of the Visigoths north of the Danube.

The alarmed Visigoths rallied an army and marched north to meet the Huns at the Dniester River. Again the Huns beat the defenders viciously, their deft horsemanship confusing the Goth armies. Surviving Visigoths fell back to the Danube and begged for permission to cross the river into the empire.

The Roman Emperor Valens, whose energy was well exceeded by his stupidity, granted the request at a hard price. Rather than accepting the Visigoths as allies against the Huns, Valens made sure the Goths entered the empire with little better than slave status. He demanded that all Visigoths who crossed the Danube surrender their arms and give up their children as hostages for good conduct. Most of these children, both boys and girls, were forced into prostitution. That the Visigoths agreed to these hard conditions speaks eloquently of the terror the Huns had inspired.

Although many Goths managed to keep some weapons, they had to endure the pain of seeing their children enslaved and were cruelly taken advantage of by the Romans. Driven by hunger, some Goths were forced to pay ten pounds of silver for a joint of meat or a loaf of bread. Gothic children not already held hostage did not keep their freedom for long. The Romans, by threatening the parents with bondage, could take the children as the price of freedom.

Too proud to endure such treatment long, the Goths soon began planning revolt. They named Fritigern to lead them, but a Roman general, hearing about the plan, plotted to kill Fritigern at a banquet. The Goth, however, escaped unharmed and roused his people to war.

The Gothic revolt first erupted in Thrace, the province just west of Constantinople. Villages were looted, livestock slaughtered, peasants murdered, buildings burned.

The Emperor Valens panicked. In the year 378, just six years after the Huns had crossed the Volga, Valens

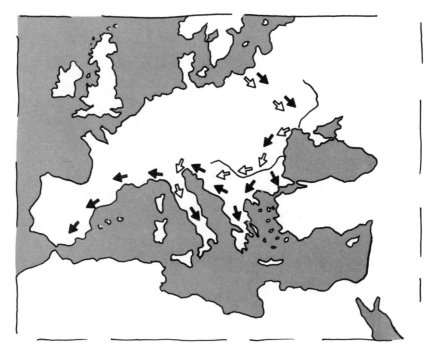

Although the migrations of the Visigoths (black arrows) and Ostrogoths began in Scandinavia, they led far into southern Europe, filling the power vacuum left by the collapse of the Roman Empire.

marched against the Goths, leading a hastily organized, inadequate force. The armies met on the plains of Hadrianople. The Roman force, made up mostly of foot soldiers, was no match for the mounted Goths, who used tactics recently learned from the Huns. The Roman defeat was so complete that the battle set a pattern for all warfare for the next thousand years. Henceforth, battles would be won not by foot soldiers but by mounted warriors.

Two-thirds of the Roman army perished. Seriously wounded, Valens and his aides sought refuge in a farm cottage. The Goths set fire to the building and Valens and his companions died in the flames.

The Goths laid siege to Constantinople. Although they were unable to break through the city's defenses, they held all other territory south of the Danube at their mercy.

Little mercy was shown. Joined by some roving bands of
Huns, the Visigoths and the Ostrogoths plundered and
destroyed from the shores of the Black Sea all the way to
the borders of Italy. Italy itself was torn by revolt.

The Gothic devastation continued until Theodosius I
took charge in Constantinople and introduced a wiser
policy. Realizing he could not beat the Visigoths and their
allies, Theodosius purchased peace with payment of tribute. Next he persuaded many Gothic warriors to join
Roman legions and work for restoration of confidence in
a badly shaken empire.

Theodosius's first major campaign was against the
rebels in Italy. He led a mixed army of barbarians, including Goths and Huns. Among his generals were the Vandal
Stilicho and the Goth Alaric, both of whom were to play
leading roles in the final acts of empire.

It Italy, Theodosius and his barbarians defeated the
general Maximus, who had falsely claimed the throne.
Valentian II, Theodosius' young half-brother, was left in
charge of the western provinces. But the boy was inadequate for the job. He lost control to his power-hungry
aides and was eventually assassinated.

Theodosius returned to Italy for another victorious
campaign. This time he put his sons in power, Honorius
in Rome in the West and Arcadius in Constantinople in
the East. Then, in Milan, exhausted by warfare and the
duties of office, Theodosius died. The year was 395 A.D.

The sons, lacking ability, soon lost control to sub-
ordinates. In the west, Stilicho took control and made the
mistake of dismissing all the Goths from his army. For the
restless Goths, fighting had become a way of life. They
elected Alaric their leader and clamored for action.

Alaric immediately led his army on a profitable campaign in Greece where they enslaved the women, killed the men of fighting age, and plundered at will. Athens, one of the few cities to escape, did so by giving the marauders all moveable wealth that the citizens could gather outside the city gates.

Stilicho tried to rescue Greece, but he began his campaign too late. He was, however, able to negotiate a truce with Alaric. Peace lasted four years, time enough for the Goths to prepare for new campaigns. In 401, Alaric led his army into Italy.

Refugees fled before the invaders. Many sought safety in southern Italy or Sicily. Stilicho had difficulty in mustering an army, but finally he met the invaders at Pollentia. The battle was still undecided when Alaric began an orderly retreat toward Rome.

With Stilicho still in the field and no other force available, Rome could not be defended. Alaric probably could have captured the city without losing a man. But he held back, perhaps out of respect for the empire. And when the Romans offered a huge bribe, he agreed to leave Italy.

Soon after the Visigoths marched out, a leader named Radagaisus led a mixed band of some two hundred thousand invaders, including Vandals and Ostrogoths, into Italy. Stilicho, at the head of a much smaller force, managed just the same to scatter the poorly organized barbarians before they could do great damage. Radagaisus was captured and brought before the Emperor Honorius in chains.

Although Stilicho had defended Rome successfully for twenty years, the emperor distrusted the Vandal. Advisors in court encouraged the distrust, suggesting that Stilicho had let Alaric escape. Actually, the advisors were jealous of the Stilicho's success and fearful of his growing power. They repeatedly reminded the emperor that the general was a Vandal. His true loyalty was not with Rome. The record spoke otherwise, but Honorius finally agreed that Stilicho should be killed.

The general, who thoroughly understood Rome's "civilized ways," did not resist the imperial executioners. Despite the protests of his friends, Stilicho knelt and bared his neck for the sword. Within a few days of his death, Honorius ordered the murder of thousands of Stilicho's barbarian followers, including most of the Roman army's most able leaders. The bloodbath was an open invitation to Alaric.

He promptly led his army back into Italy. This time nothing could stop him. Some thirty thousand of Stilicho's soldiers deserted Rome to join the Goths. Later, while laying siege to Rome, the Goth's ranks grew again when thousands of slaves fled from their masters to join the siege. It had become a highly mixed force—Huns, Visigoths, Ostrogoths, Vandals, and now slaves.

The army closed off all the supply routes to the city. Romans began to starve. Cannibalism had begun when the city sent a delegation to Alaric to seek terms. The Romans claimed that a million citizens would resist the barbarians. Alaric replied:

"The thicker the hay, the more easily it is mowed."

Eventually, Alaric agreed to withdraw if Rome paid a ransom of thirty thousand pounds of silver, five thousand pounds of gold, three thousand furs, four thousand silk tunics, and three thousand pounds of pepper, then a highly valued spice. Rome might once again have escaped had not Sarus, one of the Gothic generals, defected to Honorius with a large body of soldiers. Sarus's force attacked Alaric's main army. Alaric, seeing the attack as a violation of the truce he had tried to negotiate, attacked Rome again. A slave opened the gates for the invaders, who rushed into the city to begin an orgy of plunder, murder, and rape. The year was 410. Rome's eight-century record of invincibility had come to an end.

Alaric tried to keep his army in check, but many, particularly the Huns and the escaped slaves, were almost impossible to control. Blood flowed in the streets for four days. Only those who gained sanctuary in the churches escaped.

When Alaric finally restored order, he led his army south with thousands of captives, including Honorius's half-sister, Placidia. The Goths planned to plunder Italy and Sicily, but when they reached the "toe" of the Italian boot, Alaric died of fever. Slaves were ordered to divert a river and dig a grave in the dry river bed. When Alaric's body was laid to rest, the diversion dam was broken so that the river returned to its old channel and hid the grave. Then, to make sure the location remained a secret, the slaves who built the dam and dug the grave were killed.

Ataulf, Alaric's brother-in-law, was named king of the Visigoths. The new leader, who claimed that he wished to save rather than destroy the empire, promised peace with Rome on the condition that southern Gaul be declared the Visigoth's realm and that Placidia be his bride. Honorius agreed to cede the territory, including Bordeaux, Toulouse, and Narbonne, but he refused to let his half-sister marry the Gaul. Placidia, however, was in love. She welcomed the marriage and Honorius's protests were ignored.

By the year 414, Ataulf and his new bride began to

settle the Visigoths' new territory. Although Ataulf was assassinated a year later, Placidia continued to rule. And when Honorius died in 423, she took charge of the whole Western Empire and ruled well for twenty-five years.

Although many Ostrogoths had taken part in Alaric's campaigns in Italy, most of them remained in the east, subject to the rule of the Huns. These Goths were to play a final, tragic chapter in the fall of empire. The tragedy was theirs as much as it was Rome's.

When Attila died in 453, the Ostrogoths in his realm regained their freedom and their fighting spirit. Ostrogoth warriors were hired by the emperor at Constantinople to drive other barbarian tribes out of the Byzantine realm. The cautious emperors, however, to make sure of Ostrogoth loyalty, had the habit of keeping hostages. One of these was Prince Theodoric, who was taken into the Byzantine court when he was seven years old.

Although Theodoric apparently received little formal education, he learned a great deal about philosophy and the arts, including the art of government. In eleven years in Constantinople, his curiosity and intelligence gained the respect of the Byzantine court. And when King Theodemir, Theodoric's father, died, the youth's claim to the Ostrogoth crown was supported by Constantinople.

Some in court, however, feared that Theodoric's popularity and ability might cause trouble for the Eastern Empire. One of these was Zeno, who became emperor soon after Theodoric inherited his crown. Zeno suggested that the Ostrogoths take Italy.

Theodoric welcomed the suggestion. It would at last give his people lands of their own. Zeno, however, had other motives. The west, at the moment, was being ruled

An Ostrogoth cloak pin, believed to date from the fifth century, may have been worn by one of Theodoric's followers. The intricate pattern of inlaid stones shows a high level of craftsmanship.

by Odoacer, a barbarian of uncertain background, who had overthrown the Roman emperor and put himself on the Western throne. Although he always spoke of Zeno as the supreme ruler, Odoacer actually ignored any authority but his own. Zeno decided that sending Theodoric to Italy would not only get the Ostrogoths out of the way in the east, but might also remove the troublesome Odoacer in Italy.

In the year 488, Theodoric led twenty thousand warriors across the Alps. Although he was an Arian, Theodoric gained the support of the Roman bishops, who saw him as a representative of the Orthodox East. This support helped the Ostrogoths in their tough, five-year campaign against Odoacer's army. Finally, when Odoacer was ready to talk truce, Theodoric invited him and his son to a banquet. There, with his own sword, the Ostrogoth killed father and son, and virtually ended further resistance in the Italian peninsula.

Despite his treacherous beginning, Theodoric was to give the west one of the most orderly and prosperous reigns it had enjoyed in years. Although he extended his realm to include most of the Balkans and Sicily, he carefully remained subordinate to Constantinople.

And, as a diplomatic gesture, he often asked for guidance from the Roman senate, which had long been an ineffective body. Furthermore, he supported Roman laws, institutions, and monuments. He allowed most duties of government and the law courts to remain in Roman hands. He saw that his own Goths were well paid, but limited them to police and military duties. The Goths also received a third of Italy's farmland, the other two-thirds remaining in Roman ownership. He even ransomed Romans who had been held captive in other lands and resettled them on Italian soil. Marshes were drained and damage to buildings done by previous invaders was repaired. All these measures encouraged prosperity and reduced prices. The cost of food alone under Theodoric's reign reportedly dropped by one third.

Theodoric did not let his Arianism get in the way of religious tolerance. While he supported the Catholic church, he also encouraged free worship for all faiths. He had one of his ministers, Casiodorus, a Catholic, write:

"We cannot command religion, for no one can be forced to believe against his will."

Unfortunately, the policy was far too modern for most other religious thinkers of the day. Late in his reign, after mobs had destroyed Jewish synagogues in Milan, Genoa, and Rome, Theodoric ordered the buildings replaced at public expense. This outraged the Catholic church and a majority of Roman citizens. Riots had to be suppressed.

Meanwhile, Constantinople issued a ruling that no Arians, with the exception of Goths, could hold public office. Barbarians forced from office by the ruling appealed to Theodoric for support. Suspecting that the Gothic exception was certain to be withdrawn after his death, he protested to Constantinople, saying:

"To pretend dominion over the conscience is to usurp the prerogative of God. By nature of things the power of sovereigns is confined to political government; they have no right of punishment except over those who disturb the public peace. The most dangerous heresy is that of a sovereign who separates himself from part of his subjects because they believe not according to his belief."

This noble plea was ignored, and Theodoric himself, growing old and fearing the future, uncovered a Roman plot to replace him. He reacted by executing some of the suspects on very thin evidence. Among those killed by his order was Boethius, a popular member of the senate and the best writer of his day. Two years later, in 526, still remorseful over Boethius's death, Theodoric himself died. For thirty-four years, he had given what was left of the Roman Empire peace and by far the best government it would see for centuries to come.

Theodoric had chosen a grandson, Athalaric, to succeed him, but the boy was just ten when Theodoric died. His mother, Amalasuntha, ruled in his stead, and when the boy died at eighteen, she invited a cousin, Theodahad, to rule with her. He took sole possession of the throne and put the queen in prison. While there, she sent an appeal to Constantinople.

A Byzantine army came, not to rescue Amalasuntha

A bronze medallion made in the sixth century may have depicted one of the last Visigoth warriors.

but to rid Italy of the Ostrogoths. It proved a difficult and costly mission. The country was ravaged by eighteen years of civil war that emptied the treasury at Constantinople, destroyed everything and more of what Theodoric had rebuilt, left Rome so weak it could not defend itself, and destroyed the Ostrogoths as a distinct people.

Soon after the remnants of the Ostrogoth army marched from Italy into oblivion, the Lombards, a Germanic tribe from what is now Hungary and Austria, marched in unopposed to occupy much of northern Italy, where their heirs remain to this day.

Chapter Five

The Vandals

About five hundred years before the birth of Christ, a tribe of hardy northerners moved from northern Jutland, now Denmark, south into the fertile valley of the Oder River where they settled with other northern migrants.

The tribe prospered, its numbers grew, and by the third century A.D., the Vandals, as they were called, had a secure hold on a territory that is now known as Prussia. Early in the fourth century, however, they began to move south again.

We do not know the reason for this migration. Throughout their history, the Vandals showed a restless nature, and perhaps it did not take much pressure from other prospering tribes to set them off in search of new land. In any case, the Huns cannot be blamed. The Vandals migrated into Visigoth territory north of the Danube well before the Huns crossed the Volga.

The Vandals hardly had time to plant their crops when the Visigoths attacked them. The newcomers were

so soundly beaten that their leaders asked the Emperor
Constantine for permission to cross the Danube and settle
in Pannonia. Hoping that the Vandals would boost crop
production and help stabilize his frontier, Constantine
consented.

It was a safe gamble. Thanks to the Visigoths, the
Vandals were a beaten people. Most of their surviving
warriors were wounded or simply too exhausted to cause
trouble. And indeed, there was no trouble for seventy
years. But the Vandals were not by nature peaceful. As
the years of calm passed, the population increased, vigor
was restored, and the old restlessness returned.

During this time, the Vandals' first general was born.
His full name was Flavius Stilicho, and as we have seen, he
served Rome brilliantly and faithfully. He rose to become
leader of the western army under the Emperor Theodosius I. His rapid promotion may have been partly due
to his marriage to Theodosius's niece, but there was no
questioning the Vandal's military genius. Again and again,
he defeated larger armies less disciplined and poorer prepared than his. Stilicho won Theodosius's trust so completely, that it was the emperor's dying wish that the
Vandal serve as regent for Honorius, the young heir to the
throne.

In 395, however, the year Theodosius died, Stilicho
was sent to Greece to campaign against the marauding
Visigoths. The truce that ended that campaign allowed
Stilicho to return to Italy, but he was not finished fighting
barbarian invaders. Alaric, as we have seen, was his most
serious adversary, but as long as Stilicho remained in
charge of the legions, Alaric and his Visigoths spared
Rome.

Stilicho was the West's major military asset. The

Success and popularity were the undoing of Stilicho, but when a jealous emperor ordered the Vandal killed, his death was the undoing of the empire. This portrait follows an ivory plaque depicting the Vandal general.

Romans loved him. They put up his statue in the forum. The inscription praised his bravery and fidelity and spoke of the "exceptional love" the people had for him. No other barbarian ever received as much praise from Rome.

But the man could not save the empire alone. In 406, he was forced to call home the legions who had been defending the banks of the Rhine River, then the frontier of empire in Gaul. On the last night of that year, the Vandal tribes and their allies, the Alani and the Suevi, crossed the river into the territory now left undefended.

Thus, while one Vandal devoted the last days of his life to the defense of Rome, others launched a campaign of pillage, rape, and slaughter that would stun the world. To this day, the memory of their terror survives in the word "vandalism."

Mainz was the first large city to fall to the onslaught. After looting and slaughtering many of the city's citizens, the Vandals turned north into Belgica where they destroyed Trier. Reims, Amiens, Arras, and Tourni were left in flames. No one opposed them. They turned south into the heart of Gaul. Town after town fell until the Vandals arrived at Toulouse. There the Bishop Exuperius organized a heroic defense that saved the town, but few others escaped the Vandal fury.

The Roman poet Orientius described the devastation:

"See how swiftly death comes upon the world and how many peoples the violence of war has stricken . . . . Some lay as food for the dogs; others were killed by the flames that licked their own homes. In the villages and country houses, in the fields and the countryside, on every road— death, sorrow, slaughter, fires, and lamentation. All Gaul smoked in one great funeral pyre."

The Franks, the barbarian people who had been steadily gaining power in Gaul, put up a strong defense against the Vandals and did not allow them to settle down peacefully anywhere, but the Franks had to fight without help from the Roman legions. The legions were busy fighting the Visigoths in Italy, and they were soon to lose their dynamic leader.

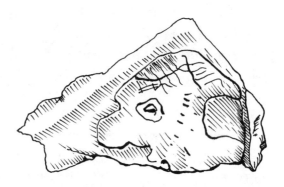

Although the Romans held military and political control in Gaul, they did not control the spirit of the people. This caricature of a fifth-century Roman official crudely suggests that some peasants may have welcomed the Vandal conquest.

Stilicho was killed by imperial order in 408. A year later one hundred thousand Vandals, tired of harassment from the Franks, crossed the Pyrenees into Spain. Behind them, Gaul lay in smoldering ruins.

Although then one of Rome's richest provinces, Spain could not defend its cities. As they had in Gaul, the Vandals killed and plundered without restraint, and they also upset a regime that had long been vulnerable.

For years, a few Romans, the owners of huge estates, had ruled a large and dissatisfied population of slaves and poor freemen. The arrival of the Vandals freed the poor from the Roman yoke. Many slaves and serfs joined the slaughter, unleashing resentment upon their former masters with at least as much cruelty as the invaders.

Merida, Cartagena, Cordova, Tarragona, Seville, and many other rich cities fell to the attackers. In just two years, the Vandal terror spread to the Straits of Gibraltar.

In the meantime, Rome fell to the Visigoths and made the truce that allowed them to settle in southern Gaul. There the Visigoths became players in the struggle for control of Spain. The Emperor Honorius offered to pay any Visigoth general who would lead an army into Spain to restore order.

Wallia, then king of the Visigoths who had settled in southwest Gaul, accepted the offer. There were other incentives than Roman gold. The Visigoths and the Vandals, as we have seen, were old enemies, and a campaign in Spain was bound to yield plunder for the victors.

Whatever their motives, the Visigoths planned and executed their attack well.

They split the Vandal army, driving the Suevi, its strongest allied group, into northwest Spain. The Vandals themselves were driven south into Andalusia.

Then the Visigoths, their military goals accomplished, established themselves as new rulers of Spain. They were soon joined by other Visigoths from southern Gaul in yet another wave of migration, caused this time by pressure from the land-hungry Franks.

The Visigoths, as we shall see, ruled Spain until the arrival of the Arabs early in the eighth century. It was during the Visigoth period that the marriage of Germanic and Latin languages gave us the Spanish that is now spoken so extensively in both the Old and New Worlds.

The Vandals, though far from beaten, realized they could no longer stay in Spain. There was no purpose in fighting their old enemy. But they were trapped in the southern end of a peninsula, looking at the sea. Where could they go?

Fortunately for the Vandals, they had a new king who had the solution to the problem.

Gaiseric was the illegitimate son of the late King Godigiselsus. His mother was a slave. Although born with a limp, the boy was strong, and grew into an able leader. His enemies called him proud, quick-tempered, cruel, and shrewd. He was perhaps all these things, but he was also the most dynamic and imaginative leader the Vandals, or perhaps any of the barbarian tribes ever had.

He began his reign by building ships and turning his land-based warriors into sailors. His goal was North Africa.

There, the Roman defenses were even weaker than they had been in Spain, and internal strife, due largely to the Donatist heresy, had made the African provinces especially vulnerable. In fact, some accounts have it that the Vandals were invited to North Africa by Boniface, the Roman governor, who reportedly needed help to defeat a political rival.

The amazing and destructive path of the Vandals led them from the protection of empire north of the Danube, westward across the Rhine and then south through Gaul and into Spain where they turned to seafaring, migrated to North Africa, and became feared pirates of the Mediterranean. Their sack of Rome in 455 A.D. was a massive pirate raid.

As events developed, however, it is difficult to believe this story.

In 429, just a year after taking power, Gaiseric led the newly launched Vandal fleet across the Straits of Gibraltar to Africa. His band, including women and children as well as warriors, numbered some eighty thousand. Compared with the eight million then living in Roman North Africa, the Vandal force seemed terribly outnumbered.

To improve the odds, Gaiseric at once put his diplomatic skills to work. The Moors, long suppressed by Roman rule, soon agreed to join the Vandals, and so, too, did many of the Donatists. Rome had recently taken away the Donatists's rights to own land. They had a score to settle. In the Arian Vandals, Donatists saw others who had suffered from Rome's religious intolerance. The two peoples shared a fellowship.

Responsible for the defense of the province, Boniface could find few men willing to fight. He was forced to retreat before Gaiseric's growing horde. The Roman legions finally made a stand at Hippo where they were joined by a band of citizen defenders organized by Bishop Augustine, the church's leading philosopher and writer of his age. In his *Confessions, City of God*, and many other books, Augustine laid the theological foundations of faith. He achieved sainthood soon after his death.

The Vandal siege of the town began in 430 and continued for fourteen months. All seemed lost for the embattled citizens when the heroic bishop died, but the Vandals suddenly broke the siege. Gaiseric withdrew his troops to meet and vanquish another Roman army. Rome begged for peace. Ambassadors for Valentinian, then the emperor, agreed to recognize Gaiseric as the ruler over most of what is now Algeria and Tunisia, making him master of every city except Carthage. For his part, Gaiseric agreed to be an ally of Rome in the treaty that was signed at Hippo on February 11, 435.

Gaiseric broke the treaty before the ink was dry by launching a fleet of pirate ships which was soon challenging Rome's authority over the Mediterranean Sea.

The pirates not only attacked merchant ships, but they also raided rich port cities. It was common in these raids for the pirates to land a small band of cavalry that attacked and swiftly destroyed or at least diverted any land defenses that might stand in the way of plunder.

Ports in Spain, Greece, and southern Italy were especially vulnerable to Vandal attack, but the pirates might appear anywhere. As Gaiseric expanded his fleet, the attacks became more frequent.

But far more devastating than pirate raids was Gaiseric's control of the North African grain crop. Rome had long relied upon African grain. Now, by withholding it, Gaiseric could blackmail Rome into accepting unfavorable treaties, granting concessions, or simply giving up territory.

The Arian Vandals never forgot their religious difference with Rome. In lands under Vandal rule, many Catholics were tortured and killed for their faith. The more famous victims are listed among the Christian martyrs of their age.

Apart from religious differences, life in Vandal territory was stable. The Vandals used the Roman model to rule North Africa. The large estates were left in charge of Roman administrators for the Vandal knew that grain and other important crops needed a climate of peace. But under Gaiseric's long rule, the Vandals never stopped wanting more territory.

On October 19, 439, he disregarded his treaty with Rome completely and took Carthage in a surprise attack. Shops were looted; storehouses were ransacked. Nobles who would not reveal real or imagined caches of wealth were tortured without mercy. Catholic priests and bishops were pulled from their churches and tortured to death. Arian clergymen were installed in their places. Rome could do nothing to save Carthage, but Constantinople made an effort. In 440, after a Vandal fleet raided Sicily and destroyed Byzantine property, the emperor of the East prepared a large fleet to clear the sea of pirates. Soon after the fleet sailed, however, Huns crossed eastern frontiers. The fleet was recalled to defend Constantinople.

It seemed that nothing could hold the Vandals in check. But Gaiseric did respect Aetius, the Roman general who followed Stilicho and was almost as brilliant. It was Aetius, remember, who would lead the combined Roman-Visigoth force that turned back the Huns in 451.

But four years after that victory, Aetius was to follow Stilicho in tragic death. The Emperor Valentinian III, who ruled the West with bad judgment and poor advice, acted on a sudden impulse of jealousy, snatched up a knife from his banquet table, and killed the general.

The inevitable then happened. Valentinian was assassinated by Aetius's friends. Political chaos followed.

It was an invitation to the Vandals. Within weeks of the assassination, Gaiseric landed near Rome and led his bloodlusting warriors into the city. The plunder and destruction lasted fourteen days. It was far worse than any of Rome's previous disasters. And when the Vandals left the smoking ruins, they took away the Empress Eudoxia and her two daughters as hostages.

Vandal raids continued unchecked.

In 460, an attempt to punish the Vandals was made by the Emperor Marjoran, who then ruled the West. He landed in North Africa, met Gaiseric's army, and was defeated. Marjoran was deposed a year later.

In 467, Leo, the emperor in the East, sent a large force against the Vandals. Led by Basiliscus, Leo's brother-in-law, the Byzantine fleet sailed head-on into the Vandal navy. Half of Leo's ships were left burning. He recalled what was left of his expedition.

Leo died in 474 and was replaced by Zeno, who was humiliated by Vandal raids in Greece. To stop the raids, he agreed to recognize the Vandals as a nation. In 476,

Zeno signed a treaty which described the Vandal kingdom as including all of Roman North Africa, the Balearic Islands, Corsica, Sicily, and Sardinia. For his part, Gaiseric promised to release all Roman prisoners without ransom and to allow Catholic clergymen to return to their former positions.

This time, the Vandal king apparently kept his side of the bargain, but he never did appoint a bishop to the long-vacant post in Carthage.

It turned out that Gaiseric's kingdom was nothing more than separate nations held together by his leadership. For when he died on January 25, 477, after forty-nine years of rule, the kingdom began to crumble. A son, Huneric, lacked the authority and skill to hold the nations together. Perhaps if there had been a new world for Vandal conquest, the kingdom might have survived. But it was not to be.

In 533, when the Emperor Justinian sent a Byzantine army to take Carthage, the Vandals had almost ceased to exist as a distinct people. The city fell after nothing more than token resistance. The Vandals' remarkable story was over.

They left no art or literature, and their mark on history was a bloody one. But the Vandals played a strategic role in the restless age. Their aggressive migration through Gaul and Spain and into North Africa forced Rome to loosen its hold on other, more distant provinces. Britain, as we shall see, was abandoned.

Chapter Six

The Anglo-Saxons

Although many Britons prospered under Roman rule, there was one large group of people who suffered—the peasants. Many of these people once had small land holdings, but they were gradually bought out by the ruling class. Without property of his own, the British peasant could become a tenant farmer or move to one of the growing towns to seek employment. In either case, his existence was meager. Most slaves were better fed.

As the years passed, the ruling Romans and the British landowners grew richer and richer. Some of the aristocracy lived in large houses that even had the modern miracles of glass windows and central heating.

Cities grew and business thrived. With cheap, peasant labor, woolens were woven for a lucrative export market. The fine cloth was sold at a huge profit, fattening the purses of the rich and establishing a reputation of quality for British woolens that remains to this day.

Roman law, the orderly system of Roman government, and Roman art and literature all benefited the British aristocracy. Most of the ruling class spoke Latin. Some could read it and write it. Had Roman rule continued, Latin rather than English might have become the dominant language of the modern world.

But thanks to the restless tribes of Europe, Roman rule in Britain came to an end. Strange to say, it happened by invitation.

While Rome ruled in Britain, no more than a few legions were needed to keep the peasants under submission and prevent attack from the undefeated Picts, Celts, and Gaels. The Romans had earlier driven these native tribes into Scotland, Wales, and Ireland. British towns and cities had long been secure. It was safe to travel on the fine Roman roads. Taking this security for granted, the Romanized natives who were becoming the ruling class took no interest in military matters. If a problem should rise, the legions always took care of it.

But in the fourth century raids by natives increased. The Picts attacked from the north. The Celts attacked from Wales. The Gaels crossed the Irish sea to raid coastal villages. At first, the legions repulsed the raids, but then Rome began recalling men from its British garrisons. Roman soldiers were needed to fight the barbarians in mainland Europe.

Of course, the raids increased. The natives often carried off loot without a challenge. Vainly, British leaders appealed repeatedly for help from Rome. Few heeded the pleas. The final appeal was at least heard by the Emperor Honorius. He answered that from now on the British would have to help themselves. Roman rule in Britain thus came to an end. It was 409 A.D. Rome's fall to the Visigoths was just a year away.

Meanwhile, Vortigern, the British leader of the day, took a desperate step. He asked tribes in Northern Germany to come to Britain and put down the native raids in exchange for British land. The Germans came promptly, the Saxons from the valleys of the Elbe River, the Angles from the region of Schleswig, and the Jutes from Jutland.

History records very few individual names from this era, but Jute lore says their warriors arrived in 449 A.D. under the leadership of two brothers, called Horsa, or mare, and Hengist, or stallion. They were apparently a winning team.

An Anglo-Saxon shield ornament shows the Germanic devotion to abstract animal forms. The artists and craftsmen rarely tried to portray the actual appearance of anything.

The Germans, who had been reared with weapons in their hands, had little difficulty in turning back the raiding Picts, Celts, and Gaels. And as promised, the Germans were rewarded with tracts of land. The British hoped in this way to establish a warrior class. But before the dust had settled from the skirmishes with native raiders, the Germans began sending for their friends and relatives in the homeland. Messengers to the homeland carried exciting news. Britain was undefended. Land could be had for the taking.

Since the Age of Migration began, the Saxons, Angles, and Jutes, like most other barbarian peoples, had been struggling to defend their home territories from land-hungry hordes. With news that new land could be had for the taking, Saxons, Angles, and Jutes crossed the English Channel by the thousands.

First welcomed as defenders, they were soon seen as invaders. British soldiers, without the help and leadership of Rome, could manage little organized resistance, and the peasants, long resentful of the aristocracy, usually sided with the new arrivals.

Defense degenerated into guerrilla war, and the struggle continued for a hundred years. It destroyed almost all that the Romans had built. Town populations scattered. Travel became dangerous. Trade came to a halt. The British defenders kept losing ground. The final battle was fought in 577 A.D., at Deorham. There the victorious Germans became masters of what was to be called Angle-land or England.

Some of the defeated Britons remained to mix their culture and their blood with the new masters. Others fled to the coast of France, settling on a peninsula that would soon be known as Brittany. Still others retreated into Scotland and Wales, resisting Anglo-Saxon advances and giving rise to the legend of a heroic ruler who defended Britain from the heathen invaders.

Although King Arthur and his knights were imaginary figures, perhaps based on heroes of the period, the stories told about them reflect the spirit of a noble era forced to give way to the crude and relentless pressure of migration.

Although the Angles, Saxons, and Jutes fought together to defeat the Britons, they did not remain united long. They divided England into several small kingdoms made up of warrior-farmers. In peace, the people tilled their small farms, but when war clouds gathered, they were quick to buckle on their swords. Often they fought among themselves, struggling for territory.

When boundary disputes were more or less settled, the Jutes held the southeast thumb of the island, an area they called Kent. The Saxons ruled in Wessex, Sussex, and Essex, which together made up a large realm south of the Thames River. And the Angles formed three kingdoms to the north, East Anglia, Mercia, and Northumberland. These and several other small kingdoms were to be ruled separately for two-and-a-half centuries.

But there was a unifying force afoot.

The Christian conversion of England was gradual and, with many individuals, incomplete. Actually, conversion had begun in the last years of the Roman era when a Celtic Church had been organized. The King Arthur stories tell how he and his knights fought to defend the Christian faith against the barbarian invaders. What really happened under the Anglo-Saxons was that the Celtic Church went undercover. It lacked the strength to fight the invaders and thus became a secret organization.

Some Saxons, Angles, and Jutes may have been introduced to Arianism, but they had not accepted it. When they arrived in Britain, most still worshipped the Norse

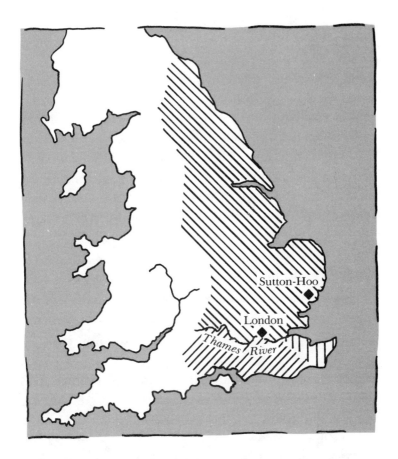

The Saxons settled south of the Thames River. The Jutes occupied territory just to the east in what is now Kent. And the Angles took control of lands to the north. The west and far north remained under Celt control.

gods. They buried their dead in the pagan way, with many grave goods furnished for the afterlife.

Marriage was hardly sacred. In fact, by today's standards most Anglo-Saxon children would be called illegitimate. Infidelity was the rule rather than the exception. If he wished, a man could sell his wife and children into slavery.

Law among the Anglo-Saxons followed the old traditions of wergild and ordeal. If a man inflicted an inch-long wound he was required to pay the victim two sheep. If a man cut off another's ear, the penalty was thirty sheep or something else of equal value. There were specific penalties for every crime imaginable. The penalty for murder varied according to the importance of the victim. Killing a king was thus judged one hundred times worse than killing a peasant. If guilt were uncertain, it was determined by ordeal. When an accused person sank in water, he or she was believed innocent. Sometimes all you had to do to prove innocence was to thrust your hand in boiling water and pick up a pebble from the bottom of the tub. A walk across hot coals was another test of innocence. Those who couldn't make the walk faced punishment.

Depending on the severity of the crime, punishment might mean the amputation of a nose, ear, hand or foot. Often criminals were sold into slavery. In severe cases the penalty was death by hanging, beheading, burning, stoning, or drowning.

Early in the Anglo-Saxon era there were many small farm holdings, individually owned and managed as family business. The family, however, did not live on its holdings. It lived instead in a small village with other families of the neighborhood. With robber bands roaming the countryside, the village was a necessity. The farmers walked each day to and from their plots of land.

Slaves did much of the heavy work making it possible to raise crops and tend cattle without great cost. Good profits made land ownership good business. The old urge to accumulate wealth rose in Anglo-Saxon England just has it had in Roman Britain. Small farms were bought up by a growing wealthy class. More and more land was managed by tenant farmers or slaves.

The wealthy Anglo-Saxon was hardly civilized. The country was noted for its heavy drinking and eating, rude manners, loose morality, and crime. It was not a friendly climate for Christian ethics. Indeed, the Celtic Church all but abandoned the hope of converting Anglo-Saxons. But the church in Rome accepted the challenge.

In the year 596, Pope Gregory sent a mission of some forty monks to England. The brave venture was headed by Augustine, a Benedictine scholar and dynamic leader (and no relation to the Bishop of Hippo). Augustine persuaded Aethelbert, king of the Jutes, to donate land to the Church at Canterbury in the heart of Kent. Aethelbert's generosity was undoubtedly influenced by his wife, Bertha, the Christian daughter of a Frankish king.

Other Germanic rulers were not so sympathetic, and the Celtic Christians, whose ritual and worship was stricter, resented the more indulgent Roman faith.

Augustine and his fellow monks had many setbacks, but in 626, the monk Paulinus achieved a major conversion. King Edwin, Angle ruler of Northumbria, accepted Christianity, and his subjects followed the lead. One by one, other kings accepted the new faith, and the church gradually became a force in the government of the land.

Thanks in large part to Augustine's scholarly nature, the church represented much more than morality and ritual. It was the civilizing force, encouraging the study of literature, the arts, history, and language. It established schools. The church brought in famous European builders and artists to design and decorate churches and to teach their skills to English craftsmen. The church also imported teachers and scholars.

The most renowned scholar of the age, however, was the Venerable Bede who was born in 673 of Anglo-Saxon parents near Jarrow in the north of England. When he was seven, his parents placed him in the nearby Peter and

Paul Monastery where the monks raised him and educated him. Bede's energy and unending curiosity made him a prize student. His interests extended everywhere, and he soon began compiling his knowledge in well-constructed Latin. He wrote on grammar, science, mathematics, and theology. He wrote a chronological history of the world and, his most famous volume, *Church History of the English Nation,* remains an important source for scholars.

By the time of his death in 735, Bede was known throughout Europe for his scholarship and facile pen. He was the best product of the church's early work in England. Often, that work had proved disappointing.

Archeological evidence shows that conversion was a two-way street. Even after conversion, many Anglo-Saxons continued to follow old burial practices, furnishing graves with weapons, jewels, and other valuables. Some burials suggest that some chieftains abandoned the new faith entirely in favor of the old gods.

Many pagan burials have been discovered, but the most famous came to light at Sutton Hoo on the Suffolk coast in 1939 when a large oblong mound was excavated. The remains of a wooden rowing ship some 86 feet long were discovered. It proved to be a treasure ship laden with coins, jewelry, plates, bowls, and weapons. There was no body in the burial, but scholars believe the treasure ship was buried between 650 and 660 A.D. as a memorial to a dead king whose body was lost. Historical records suggest that the king was Aethelhere, an East Anglia ruler whose body was washed away in a river flood after he had been killed in battle. Whoever the king was, he was much respected by his people. The weapons and the jewelry provide some of the best and richest examples of Anglo-Saxon craftsmanship known today.

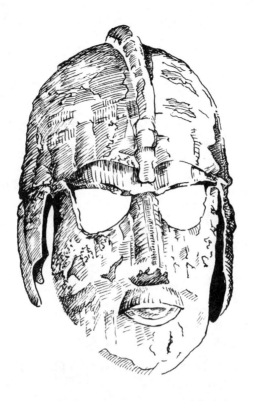

An iron helmet once covered with strips
of silver and bronze is one of the treasures
found in the Sutton-Hoo burial.
This may have actually been a portrait
of the dead king.

The pagan burial at Sutton Hoo strongly suggests backsliding among the converted royalty. Certainly, the church's early work was not easy, and though it always preached peace and unity, it could not claim much credit for the first unification of England.

That feat was achieved in 829 by Egbert of Wessex who apparently relied more on trickery and the Saxon force of arms than on the teachings of the church. And unity was short-lived. The Angles, Saxons, and Jutes were soon once again arguing and fighting among themselves.

When more permanent unity finally came, it was

partly a reaction to the Vikings. But much credit must also go to the leadership of one heroic Anglo-Saxon king. The Viking raiders, sometimes Norwegians but more often Danes, were first reported in 787, when three ships landed on the Wessex coast. An old chronicle reports that these were "the first ships of Danish men that sought land of Engle folk."

Other raids followed. In 793, the Danes sacked a monastery and killed all its monks. A year later, they pillaged Wearmouth and Jarrow in Northumberland. Kent and East Anglia were attacked in 838, and in 839, a fleet of three hundred and fifty Viking longboats anchored in the Thames River. The pillaging and slaughter ranged from London to Canterbury.

The raiders overran Northumberland in 867 and claimed it as Viking territory. The Danish conquest of England had begun. In 871, when the Danes ruled almost all lands north of the Thames, they marched on Reading, the Wessex capital. A Saxon army, led by King Ethelred and his young brother, Alfred, met the Danes. The Saxons turned the invaders back in the battle of Ashdown, but when the two armies met again, Ethelred was fatally wounded. The Saxons fled.

Alfred, at twenty-two, inherited the Wessex throne. Reports say he was subject to epileptic fits, and when he began his reign, he apparently could not read or write. A month after becoming king, he led his few followers against the Danes and lost so completely that he had to pay the enemy to leave him in peace. Despite his handicaps and early setbacks, Alfred became the greatest leader Anglo-Saxon England would have.

He gradually strengthened his army and gathered allies until, in 878, he was able to face the Danes again.

The battle of Edington was a decisive victory for Alfred. It brought peace and an agreement from the Danes to pull back into northern England.

Alfred then began rebuilding the country. He brought East Anglia, Mercia, and Wessex under his protection. He reorganized his government, strengthened his army, and began building a navy. He ordered the restoration of old buildings and the construction of many new ones to house government offices. He maintained the value of coinage, following a tradition that had already made Anglo-Saxon money favored over devalued Roman coins throughout Europe. He insisted on efficient administration of justice and made sure that the poor were protected under the law. An eighth of all royal revenues went to aid the poor.

This was one of the coins, minted by King Alfred, that helped establish preference for British currency in European trade.

Another eighth went to Alfred's favorite endeavor— education. He established a palace school at Reading and gave generously to support teaching in churches and monasteries. He imported teachers and scholars and he welcomed any traveler who could add to his knowledge of other lands. He encouraged art and commerce. And in his spare time, he taught himself to read.

When he was not struggling with the written word himself, he had others read to him. Sometimes he kept his readers busy day and night. He recognized the importance of the developing native language and ordered several books translated into English. The king himself translated at least four books. He also recorded the songs of his people and joined in singing them at his court.

The most enlightened ruler of his day, King Alfred earned the respect of other nations and built the pride of his own people. He did not change their rude ways, and the number of tenant farms increased as the thanes, or nobles, added to their land holding, but meetings of these nobles became an important facet of Anglo-Saxon government. The national Witenagemot or "meeting of the wise" was the foundation for England's Parliament. Kings could not add to their personal wealth, levy new taxes, declare war, or even stay in office without consent of the Witenagemot. It was a major step toward representative government.

Near the end of Alfred's reign, a new generation of Danes began raiding the English coast. In 899, two years before he died, Alfred saw his army and his new navy turn back the raiders, but the raids continued. The Danes, often allied with Swedish Vikings, seemed to gain strength and determination. The kings who followed Alfred were often able leaders and brave warriors, but they could not stop the relentless Danes. In 1016, little more than a century after Alfred's death, the Danes won a final victory in the Battle of Assandum and became rulers of England.

Under the Danish emperor Knut or Canute, England

King Knut or Canute, shown being crowned
in a manuscript illustration, gave England
a score of peaceful years.

enjoyed twenty years of peace. But soon after he died in
1035, the English revolted and elected Edward the Confessor to the throne. The Danes tried to regain England
in 1066.

It was a busy year. Edward died leaving the throne
reluctantly to Harold Godwinsson, leader of a rival group
of nobles. He was challenged at once by two foreign
leaders. Duke William of Normandy claimed that Edward
had promised him the English crown. Harald the Hard-
Ruler of Norway, who believed in the old Viking tradition
of right through might, declared that England still was a
Norse dominion.

Harald the Hard-Ruler sailed across the North Sea leading an invasion fleet of more than three hundred long-boats. He landed in Yorkshire on September 20, 1066. Harold Godwinsson, waiting in London to see which invaders would land first, rushed his army north almost two hundred miles and surprised the Vikings at Stamford Bridge.

Most of the Vikings, including the Norwegian king, were killed, but the battle exhausted the defenders. Just the same, Harold of England led his men south to meet the Norman threat. At Hastings, nineteen days after beating the Vikings, Harold met William's army. The Normans won and Harold was killed, but it was hardly the end of Anglo-Saxon England.

True, both the Danes and the Normans contributed to the English culture and language. Politically, the invaders ruled for many years, but throughout, the country remained essentially Anglo-Saxon in character. The invaders were simply absorbed by the existing, more vigorous culture. Today, English law, government, literature, and language can all trace their primary roots to Anglo-Saxon origins.

The barbarians had built a nation.

Chapter Seven

For Love of Allah

By no imagination of the medieval mind could the dry, vast, and remote Arabian Peninsula be seen as the seat of empire. Sparsely settled, its people had long been ruled by aliens. Alexander brought Greek rule. Then came the Romans, and finally the Byzantines.

But the aliens never had firm control over the independent Arabs. Certainly, little foreign influence had affected the culture or commerce of the desert people. Most of them were nomads, herding their livestock across the highlands, moving from one oasis to the next.

Little foreign influence could reach these nomads simply because no foreigner knew how to survive the blistering heat, the sandstorms, and the waterless expanse of the Arabian Peninsula.

The world's largest, the peninsula is bordered on the west by the Red Sea and on the east by the Arabian Gulf. It is one thousand four hundred miles long and up to one thousand two hundred and fifty miles wide. Most of it is more than one thousand feet above sea level. Years can pass without rainfall. Along the Red Sea coast, however, there is enough rain to make limited farming possible. Here ancient Arabs built their towns and cities, including Medina and Mecca.

These communities were surrounded by farms where such spices as frankincense, thyme, lavender, and jasmine and such fruits as oranges, peaches, apricots, and dates were grown. Most of the city dwellers, about a twelfth of the total Arab population, were merchants. They marketed the produce of their own fields and orchards, but more importantly, they controlled the caravan route between Syria and India, long the only commercial link between eastern and western markets.

The merchants of Mecca had another important source of income. The Kaaba, an ancient shrine, drew thousands of pilgrims each year. The travelers paid well for food and lodging, and they stayed several days to worship the old gods. The Kaaba, a large stone building, housed several idols, including statues of Allah and his three daughters. But the building itself was just as sacred as the gods it housed. At one corner of the Kaaba was a reddish black stone that the faithful believed had been cast down from heaven.

No pilgrim left Mecca without kissing the stone.

There had been talk of a new faith, a belief in one god rather than many. The Christians and the Jews believed in one god and the success and endurance of their creeds impressed the Arabs, but most of them resisted the idea of change. Much of the resistance, of course, came from the merchants who had grown rich from the pilgrim trade. Any talk of change in the old beliefs was a threat to the merchant class.

The merchant class, in a sense, ruled Arabia, but it was not really a nation, not yet.

Most Arabs gave their allegiance to their clan or tribe, and there were many tribes, each with its own leader. Although it was a crime to kill another member of one's own tribe, it was no crime to kill someone outside the tribe. You could steal, too, outside the tribe but never from your own tribe. Blood feuds between the tribes were common.

How these feuding, independent people, in little more than a century, built an empire that stretched from India to Spain is one of history's most remarkable stories.

The story begins in 659 A.D. In England, the Anglo-Saxon victory at Deorham was still eight years in the future. Justinian, perhaps the most influential of all Byzantine rulers, had been dead little more than four years.

It was in Mecca that Amina, young widow of Abdallah, a merchant who had died on the way home from Medina, gave birth to a boy. The fatherless child was named Mohammed, meaning "Highly Praised." At first, he did not seem highly blessed. His mother died when he was six. The young orphan had to live with an aging grandfather and later with an uncle.

Little is known of Mohammed's early years. He apparently was given some practical education, but he was never taught to read and write. The world at that time did not deem such skills necessary.

Legends say when he was twelve he went north into Syria with his uncle on a trading expedition. Other trips apparently followed. During his travels, he is believed to have learned much from Christians and Jews about their faiths. He made at least one trip to the Syrian trade center of Bostra on behalf of Khadija, a rich widow of Mecca. A few years later he married her. She was forty. Mohammed was twenty-five. Although most Arabs of means had several wives, Mohammed took no other wife until after Khadija died twenty-six years later.

The young merchant and his wife had children, including two sons who both died in infancy. Mohammed also adopted Ali, the orphaned son of his uncle. Later Ali married Fatima, Mohammed's daughter.

Mohammed was a member of the Quaraish tribe which had ruled Mecca for many years until a recent blood feud divided authority. The chieftain Hashim, who was either Mohammed's grandfather or great-uncle, was challenged by Umayya, a nephew, who gathered many followers. Mohammed spent much of his life defending Hashimite politics, but as he grew older, he devoted more and more time to religious discussion and contemplation.

In the holy month of Ramadan it became his custom to take his family to a cave three miles from Mecca for devotion, meditation, prayer, and fasting. He experienced his first vision in the cave in the year 610 A.D. According to Moslem tradition, Mohammed was sleeping alone when the Angel Gabriel appeared to say:

"O Mohammed! Thou art the messenger of Allah, and I am Gabriel."

In the vision, the angel forced Mohammed to read. He was not only able to understand the words, but he remembered them after he woke. Thus began the revelations that the faithful believe the prophet continued to receive the rest of his life. The visions were frequent, and when they were over, he dictated his revelations to a scribe. The collection of these revelations, the "Bible" for all Moslems, is known today as the Koran, and it has become the Arab code of ethics. There are passages in it that parallel the Christian Bible and the Jewish Talmud. Indeed, Mohammed believed that the Bible and the Talmud were inspired by God. The trouble was that men had since corrupted and misinterpreted the original meanings of these works.

Mohammed claimed, for instance, that the Christian idea of the Trinity was a corruption, a return to polytheism. The Prophet declared there was but one God, Allah, and only those who believed in him alone enter paradise.

At first only Khadija believed that her husband's visions were divine revelations. But Mohammed was a compelling speaker. He opened his house to all who would hear him. First Ali accepted the faith, then Zaid, a servant in Mohammed's house. Next a kinsman, Abu Bekr became a convert and soon brought five other Quaraish leaders into the faith. Abu Bekr and his friends are known today as the "Six Companions," the chief apostles of the new faith.

Despite this early success, Mohammed had many difficulties. Most of his converts were slaves. His own tribesmen called him a half-wit and had they not feared a blood feud, they probably would have killed him or at least tested his faith with violence. The slaves, however, could be persecuted without fear of revenge.

Many of the slave converts were forced to stand in the sun without water until they renounced the new faith. Mohammed countered by saying that renouncing under force or pain did not count, but this did not stop the persecution. Soon Mohammed and most of those who, like him, followed the chieftain Hashim were ostracized. They were forced to withdraw to a special section of Mecca.

Then Khadija, his only wife and most loyal believer, died. Mohammed was devastated. He decided to leave Mecca.

In 620, with his family and a few friends, he moved to Taif, a small town sixty miles to the east. But Taif, with close commercial and political ties to the merchants of Mecca, rejected the prophet. The people shouted insults and threw stones at him. Mohammed soon returned to Mecca where he suffered two more years of harassment.

Medina, a rival city to the north, offered a haven. Many pilgrims from Medina had heard Mohammed preach at the Kaaba. They invited the prophet to their city. Mohammed hesitated, but after learning that members of the Umayya clan were plotting to kill him, he accepted Medina's invitation. He arrived there on June 16, 622, completing the *hijra* or flight that Moslems revere as the start of the new era of their faith.

The people welcomed the prophet. Some even vied for the honor of leading his camel. His mission flourished in Medina. He built a mosque and two homes for the two wives he had married since Khadija's death. Soon he married additional wives. He became the civil as well as the spiritual leader of the city. Legal disputes were brought before him for his judgment, but his main interest was the new faith. He taught the people how to pray, and he gave the new religion a name—*Islam*, which means surrender to God. Followers became known as *Muslimin* or Moslems.

The converts flocking to Medina created a shortage of food. Mohammed solved the problem by ordering raids on passing caravans. The raids became an important source of income. One-fifth of all the loot went to the new faith and its charities. The rest was retained by the raiders.

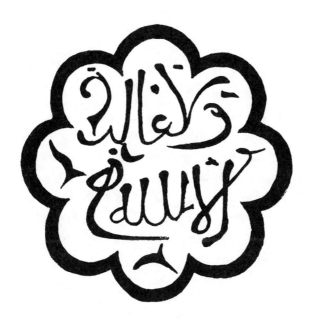

*Because the Koran said picturing people was
a form of idolatry, the artists of Islam
focused their creative talents on devotional
lettering. This says, "There is no conqueror
but God."*

Mohammed made sure that the losers from these raids
were the rich merchants of Mecca who had opposed him.

But raiding was risky. Once, when Mohammed himself led a band of three hundred to raid a rich caravan, the
merchant, with advance warning, brought an army of
nine hundred to surprise the prophet. The battle was
fought in a dry valley twenty miles south of Medina.
Despite the odds, Mohammed and his men won and returned to Medina with many prisoners and much booty.
He called his victory a miracle, the work of Allah.

Mohammed's visions continued. The written record
that was to become the Koran grew almost daily. One
important article of faith went into the record. It said
that those who died fighting for Allah went instantly to
Paradise. This simple creed turned the fighters for Islam
into fierce warriors and led to hundreds of victories.

There were, however, some military setbacks. Mohammed was seriously wounded and his army of one thousand badly beaten when it clashed with a force of three thousand from Mecca, led by the merchant Mohammed had earlier defeated. The merchant, thinking the prophet had been slain, returned victoriously to Mecca only to learn a few weeks later that Mohammed was alive and preparing for war.

At first tolerant of the many Jews in Medina, the prophet now saw them as enemies of his war plans. He drove them from the city and confiscated their property. Thus when the merchants of Mecca mounted a new offensive, many in the ranks were Jewish warriors, seeking revenge. The force, ten thousand strong, laid siege to Medina, but they could not penetrate the city's defenses. After twenty days the army withdrew. Mohammed immediately led a force against the Jewish camp, captured most of the people and gave them the choice of Islam or death. The Jews chose death. Six hundred soldiers were slain, and their women and children were sold into salvery.

Now wise in war, the prophet was Medina's military leader as well as the civil and religious leader. In his ten years in the city, he planned sixty-five campaigns and led twenty-seven of them. But he knew that continued fighting against the stronger forces from Mecca would eventually bring defeat. He asked Mecca for peace. A ten-year truce was accepted. It began in 628. A year later, Mohammed peacefully entered Mecca, leading two thousand Moslem pilgrims.

His people conducted themselves with dignity and devotion. Although they chanted their belief in one God, they still held the Kaaba holy, ignoring the fact that it housed many "pagan" idols. All Mecca was impressed.

Many, including some of the prophet's old enemies, became converts. He gained so much support that when Mohammed returned to Medina, he knew that he could now take Mecca by force.

In 630, with the truce only two years old, Mohammed led an army of ten thousand against Mecca. Leaders of the city, seeing the size of the force, opened the gates in surrender. The prophet spared all but a few of his most powerful enemies. He destroyed the Kaaba idols and declared Mecca the Holy City of Islam, a sacred place where nonbelievers must never be allowed to set foot.

His conquest of Mecca soon united all Arabia under one faith and one civil authority. Mohammed devoted himself to the problems of government and the organization of the growing faith. He sent ambassadors to foreign cities and kingdoms, preaching conversion to his faith. The king of Persia and the emperor in Constantinople were thus urged to worship Allah.

Mohammed's revelations often turned to the practical problems. One revelation even gave permission for him to marry the young wife of one of his adopted sons. By now he had ten wives and two concubines. His household was large and noisy with domestic quarrels. Although he lived a simple life, his wives desired expensive luxuries. This was the base for most of the household arguments. He rarely had the rest he needed.

At age 63, already weakened by frequent bouts of fever, Mohammed fell gravely ill. This time the fever continued fourteen days. And on June 7, 632, he died.

The prophet's death marked the beginning of Islamic conquest. Mohammed had achieved the great goal of turning a land of independent nomads into a nation with one faith and one code of ethics. Those who followed attained another goal—empire. At the beginning, they did not seek empire. They did not even dream it.

Abu Bekr, who had been the first convert outside of Mohammed's own family, was named to succeed the prophet as spiritual leader. Islam's first caliph or "representative" had no interest in expanding his realm. His major concern was revolt among tribal leaders who refused to continue paying the taxes that Mohammed had demanded. The rebels marched on Medina. Abu Bekr organized an army overnight and picked Khalid ibn al-Walid to lead it.

The new general, who soon became known as "the Sword of God," was a master of desert tactics. And he was ruthless in victory. He quickly put down the rebels and marched on to quiet dissension elsewhere in the peninsula. Then he prepared to march north where Arab tribes had long been asking for help in their struggle against the Eastern empire of Byzantium. The Byzantine soldiers, trying to enforce Greek Christian rule, had roused the hatred of all Arabs. Khalid had no difficulty in getting volunteers for his campaign.

Actually, the call for help from the northern tribes was just an excuse for aggression. The Arabs needed more land because of increasing population. There was already a food shortage during Mohammed's lifetime, now it was getting serious. And the time was ripe for attack. Persia and Byzantium had long been at war. Both sides had been so badly weakened they could no longer defend the cities and towns along the Arab border.

Early in 633 Khalid led a Moslem army of five hundred across the border into Persia. They rode all the way to the Euphrates River where, with the help of two thousand five hundred local tribesmen, they captured Hira. Abu Bekr probably did not authorize this raid, but any protests he may have raised were quieted by the loot his general sent back to Medina.

While still in Hira, Khalid received news of an Arab force in danger of defeat by a Byzantine army near Damascus five days to the west. Only Arabs knew how to survive such a journey. Before starting the waterless trek, Khalid made his camels drink to their fill. During the ride, the Arabs kept their horses alive on camel's milk. Near the end, they killed some camels for the water in their bellies. When Khalid reached the besieged Arabs, his men were exhausted. Just the same, they defeated a superior Byzantine army decisively.

Abu Bekr died before news of the victory could reach him. He was replaced by his close advisor Omar. Omar objected to Khalid's cruelty and replaced him with Abu Obeida. The new general, however, retained "the Sword of God" as military advisor.

Damascus was captured, then Antioch and Jerusalem. All of Syria was annexed in 640. A year later, Egypt and Persia were swept up in the tide of Islam. The Arab horsemen and the Arab cavalry were far swifter and better trained than any of their foes. And Arab courage could not be matched. Death in the cause of Allah was, after all, a sure and swift entry into paradise.

In the wake of victory, Arabs migrated northward by the thousands to take possession of the conquered lands. The movement was large and swift. Just four years after the first stage of conquest ended, a half million Arabs were living in Syria and Persia.

Energetic colonizers, they drained and cleared land, built irrigation systems, and cultivated new crops. Of

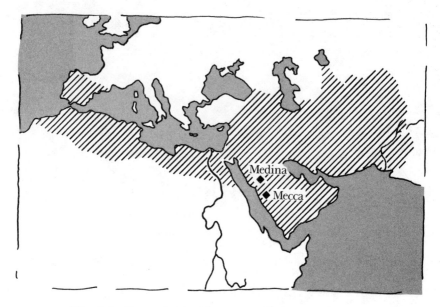

The Islamic world stretched from the Indus River across the Mideast and North Africa on into Spain.

course, some Arabs prospered at the expense of others. Wealth eventually became concentrated in the hands of a few. For native Syrians and Persians, however, the living standard was generally higher than it had been before the Arabs arrived.

Omar died in 644. He was succeeded by Othman ibn Affan, a member of the Umayyad clan that had long opposed Mohammed and his Hashimites. Civil dissent erupted. Ali, Mohammed's adopted son, who had long believed the caliphate was rightfully his, rallied an opposition party that included five hundred Egyptian pilgrims who believed Mohammed's spirit was embodied in Ali. They also believed in direct action. In Medina the pilgrims demanded Othman's resignation. When he refused, they broke into the palace and killed him. The year was 656.

Ali became caliph, but of course, he was immediately challenged by the Umayyad and all their supporters. Both sides raised armies. Ali won a key victory at Khoriaba in what is now southern Iraq, but revolt continued to fester. After making truce with one opposing army, Ali saw many of his own soldiers defect to form another dissenting force. Before achieving peace, he was killed by an assassin. In 661, Amuwija, another Umayyad leader, brought uneasy unity to the empire. He established his capital at Damascus, more centrally located than Medina, and began a rule that was far more political than spiritual, and when he died in 680, Arab blood flowed again in another war of succession.

This time the contenders for the caliphate were Amuwija's son, Yezid, and Ali's son, Husein. Both died in battle. Although three different caliphs claimed the throne, none could unify the country. Finally, Abd-al-Malik, a cousin of Amuwija showed enough courage and cruelty to win the attention and eventually the respect of most Arabs. Actually, after the rebels were subdued, Abd-al-Malik had a peaceful reign. It lasted twenty years, and it was followed by the stable rule of his four sons.

Arab conquest began anew. The warriors of Islam took north Africa and, at the invitation of warring Visigoths, invaded Spain in 712. A year later and far to the east, Arab armies captured Samarkand, a trade center little more than four hundred miles from China. They also claimed Afghanistan and a large territory of western India. Christians and Jews were tolerated in the conquered territories as long as they agreed to pay an annual tribute or tax for the privilege of living in Arab land. Those who converted to the new faith, and many did, avoided further taxation.

Arab expansion all but ended in 720 when a campaign against Constantinople fizzled. Finally at peace, the Arab empire enjoyed a long period of prosperity, cultural and scientific achievement, and a stable government that was usually just and wise. Spain and western India, although they remained Islamic, soon rejected Damascus's rule, starting a trend that would eventually produce many independent states in the Arab world.

But there were many generations of stability. Arabs had time to study, think, and create. They built a culture far in advance of any society that could be found in medieval Europe. They delighted in stories and in poetry. They pioneered in the study of astronomy, medicine, philosophy, chemistry, and mathematics. They created a distinct art, ornate and colorful. Their mosques and the public buildings were crowned with grand and graceful domes.

This playful design gives the Islamic salutation: "In the Name of God, Most Gracious, Most Merciful."

Many of the words we use today such as *caravan, check, tariff, bazaar, chemistry, alchemy,* and *magazine* are Arabic in origin.

After the Moslems were driven out of Spain, the pace of breakup quickened. When Turkey rose to power, the separate Arab states could not unite in an effective defense. Then the Mongol invasion, as we shall see, left much of the Middle East in ruins. But the faith survived. And it spread.

Today Islam is the dominant religion in the Philippines, Indonesia, Malaya, Pakistan, Afghanistan, Iran, Iraq, Syria, Jordan, Turkey, parts of China and Russia, and many countries of Africa. And new converts are added every day.

Chapter Eight

The Open Road

They were in Persia and North Africa by 1000 A.D. They arrived in Turkey by 1100. Two hundred years later, they appeared in Crete. By 1370, their colorful caravans were a common sight in the Balkan states. They first arrived in Bohemia in 1399, in Germany in 1417, in Belgium in 1420 and in France in 1427. By 1440, they had spread across England and into Wales. Later in the same century they moved into Spain and Russia. They came to the United States in 1843.

Who are they and where did they come from?

In India, where these restless wanderers originated, they are known as Banjara, Gor, or some other tribal name. Many of them are still there, enjoying a touch of prosperity after centuries of poverty and oppression.

Elsewhere, they are most commonly called the Rom or Gypsies. The French thought they came from Bohemia and thus called them Bohemians, a name that has since taken on broader definition. In England it was first thought that the roaming bands came from Egypt. They were thus called "Gypcians," a name soon changed to Gypsies.

Up until barely a hundred years ago, no one, not even the Gypsies themselves, could say where they came from. One of the first clues in solving the mystery occurred when an English Gypsy was visiting the docks in London where a tramp steamer was being loaded. The Gypsy was startled to discover that he could understand most of what the Indian crewmen were saying. Romany, the language of the Gypsies, and one of the native tongues of India, though not the same, had surprising similarities.

Today we know that racial traits and language link the Gypsy heritage firmly to northwestern India and Pakistan, but we still cannot explain with certainty what caused thousands of natives to cross the Indus River and head west one thousand years ago.

The people themselves have a legend that says it all started with a battle. The Banjara, the legend says, were so badly beaten that many of them vowed to keep wandering until their humiliation was avenged.

Some scholars believe the travels of several northwest Indian tribes began with attacks by the Sultan Mahmud of Ghazni in the eleventh century. The Sultan, famous for his ugliness as well as his ambitions, first united the Afghan-Persian Empire and then began raiding his neighbors. His armies, complete with war elephants, raided India seventeen times. Every raid brought thousands of slaves into Persia.

Could these slaves be the first of the wandering Gypsies?

Perhaps, but there's a puzzle. When the old Sultan died and his empire, under the weak hand of his son, began to crumble, why didn't the slaves return to their

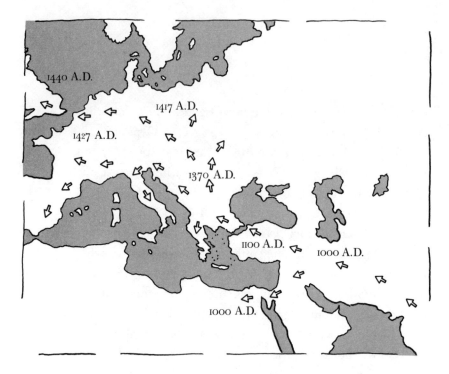

The path of Gypsy migration led from India into Persia and North Africa, then into Turkey, and from there into Europe.

native India? The Turks soon controlled the Sultan's vast empire. Wouldn't the displaced Indians have been better off at home, free, than under the Turkish rule as slaves?

Scholars who know the Indian caste system say no. The Sultan's captives who returned to India would have been regarded as escaped slaves, the lowest level in the caste system. Better they wander forever than try to go home.

While no one can say what caused the great wandering, it seems that the Banjara were wanderers long before any of them left India.

In Sanskrit, the word "Banjara" means forest dweller or wanderer, and we know that those who remained in India continued to move from one spot to the next without any permanent home. Their restless nature made them useful to the ancient rulers of India.

In times of peace the Banjara were busy traders dealing in salt, grain, and livestock. Always on the move, they supplied areas where food was short, and their free trading kept prices stable. In times of war, they were responsible for supplying the armies with food and weapons.

Their duties as noncombatant suppliers were well-documented in the seventeenth century when Asaf Khan, a great Mogul vizier, sent a copper plate engraved with gold as a gift of appreciation to Banjara chiefs who had provided a pack train of one hundred thirty thousand animals for the Khan's army. The inscription on the plate said:

"Your bullocks can drink from the pots of my followers, they can eat the thatch of their roofs. I will even allow three murders a day as long as I find your bullocks where my cavalry rides."

Yes, the wanderers were known as violent people. It was said that they drank too much too often. Their night-long parties usually ended, it was said, in bloody fights. Even their children carried lethal knives and knew how to use them, or so it was said.

It was widely believed that the bejeweled Banjara women knew all the skills of witchcraft and would cast spells on anyone who opposed them. Certainly, they could look into the future and tell fortunes. Couldn't they?

Unfortunately, many of the things said of the Banjara arose from suspicion and prejudice. Their wandering ways placed them outside traditional social and religious structures. The men never seemed to work regular hours like other people. They rarely planted crops. They wore strange, colorful clothing. Even the men sometimes wore jewelry.

They were superstitious, clannish, and secretive. They

*A Turkish shadow-puppet depicts
a scheming Gypsy with a crafty eye.
The puppet play supported the prejudice
against doing business with Gypsies.*

made their own laws. They lived apart. In Christian countries, the Gypsies were often despised as thieves, kidnappers, and pagans. Actually, Gypsies traditionally have
followed the religious practices of the host country, but
sometimes their sincerity has been questioned.

In England, for example, where church congregations
often give coins to the parents of a newly baptized baby,
Gypsies have been known to visit several different churches
on a Sunday morning, collecting perhaps a half-dozen
Christian names for a baby as well as a heavy bag of coins.

In many cases the poor reputation for honesty was
well founded. Gypsies, faced with hard times, did steal and
deal in stolen goods. Some stole whenever the opportunity
arose. And Gypsies had clever ways of hiding their loot.
Sometimes the thieves would bury it at camp and then
build a fire over the spot. Police might come and tear the
camp apart, searching for the loot, but they never found
it. Who would think of looking under a fire?

Gypsies were said to kidnap babies to raise them in
the clan. But few stories of kidnapped youngsters who grew
up to become Gypsies with no memory of any other life

can be proven. There were older children who ran away
to join Gypsy bands, but they often had trouble persuad-
ing the Gypsies to accept them.

Actually, the Gypsies's reputation as kidnappers of
children goes back to ancient rumors in India. There it
was said that the Banjara would bury a kidnapped child
up to the neck. Then they would drive their bullocks
over the spot. If the child's head were badly crushed by
the hooves of the passing cattle, it meant that the Banjara's
coming journey would be successful. If such a ritual were
practiced, it has long been forgotten. Today's Gypsies love
and respect children.

It's true that many superstitions have survived. Like
most Gypsies, the Banjara avoid white clothing, believing
that white is the color of death. It is also considered bad
luck to speak the names of the dead.

B. P. Menon, editor of the *United Nations Chronicle*,
recently attended a tribal meeting or "Panchayat" of Banjara men in India. It began like a judicial court with fines
being collected for such misdeeds as swindles or late payment of debt. Disputes were settled. New births were
registered for a fee of five rupees each. Then toward the
end of the session, a goat, paid for with part of the money
collected, was led into the circle of men.

As the angry goddess Kali was praised, cold water was
splashed on the goat, and while the animal's flank was
still quivering from the shock, its throat was slashed.
Menon said quivering of the goat's flesh was believed to
be a sign of Kali's favor. It was important to kill the animal at that moment. But the ceremony was more than
worship. The blood was symbolic of tribal unity. For the
Banjara, the old bonds had been renewed.

The Panchayat is still held once a month.

Tribal unity often made the difference between death and survival. When the British took control of India and began building a vast system of railways, the role of the Banjara as traders was eliminated. British land policies stressed cash crops rather than subsistent crops. Famines became a way of life in India, and the Banjara, deprived of their ancient profession, suffered more than any other peoples. Tribal unity was all that remained of their proud past.

Hunger drove many Banjara to full-time crime. The British, calling them a criminal tribe, restricted their movements and forced the men to carry identity cards. Other Indians, Hindus and Moslems alike, were unsympathetic and looked upon the Banjara as outcasts.

Although some took to the forests and lived by hunting, others became smiths, weavers, or other craftsmen. By selling their wares on the streets, they managed to survive.

It was not until British rule ended and the home government adopted laws to ease poverty and benefit minorities that the Banjara began to regain economic and social status. Scholarship programs have enabled Banjara people to enter the medical, legal, and other professions. But they have not given up their tribal unity or, as Menon reports, their ancient customs.

Up until World War II, Gypsies in other parts of the world also retained their unity and their ancient customs. And they kept wandering.

A few years before the war, when he was twelve, Dutch author Jan Yoors ran away with a gypsy band. He traveled through Europe in a caravan of colorful wagons with the same family for ten years. No non-Gypsy is better informed than he about Gypsy life on the road.

Many Gypsies still live in India where one of their largest tribes is known as the Banjara. Here a Gypsy mother and her children are on their way to the town well.

In his book about the experience, *The Gypsies,* Yoors describes a Gypsy meeting or *kris* which differs little from the Panchayat of the Banjara. Although there was no sacrifice, the European Gypsies did sit down to a feast after settling disputes and recording important events.

In addition to Romany, according to Yoors, the European Gypsies are able to speak many other languages they learned in their wandering. Boundaries mean little to them, and Gypsies saw no wrong in carrying forged papers or false identity cards to avoid trouble with authorities when crossing from one country into another.

There was much animosity between the Gypsy and non-Gypsy worlds. *Caje* is the derisive term for a non-Gypsy. *Gorgio* is the more polite term. Some Gypsies still find pleasure in taking advantage of the *Gorgio*, putting them in a bad light, or making them look foolish. Gypsies, after all, are a racial minority and have suffered centuries of discrimination. This has not, however, damaged their pride or their loyalty.

Yoors found that most Gypsy women told fortunes for the *Gorgio*. But they would never tell each others' fortunes. Belief in fortune-telling was considered a *Gorgio* weakness, below the dignity of any self-respecting Gypsy. And few Gypsies really deal in curses and charms. But they let the *Gorgio* believe that Gypsies had special and mysterious powers. A little fear among the *Gorgio* was a good thing. Over the centuries, *Gorgio* fear of unknown consequences have saved Gypsies from much persecution.

Gypsy bands sometimes elected a "king" to deal with the *Gorgio*, but these "kings" rarely had real authority and sometimes lacked respect. They simply fronted for the band, took what abuse might come from the non-Gypsy world, and sometimes even went to jail.

The *Gorgio* thought it severe punishment to jail the Gypsy "king," but the gypsies could shrug it off and go their own way, knowing that the jailed "king," though not greatly missed, would eventually be released and catch up with the band.

Yoors's Gypsies saw no evil in telling lies to *Gorgio*. Often it was a matter of pride not to tell the same story

The Gypsy love of colorful design is suggested by this green and white door panel from a Gypsy wagon. The picture of a horse usually meant that these Gypsies were horse traders.

twice. This was one reason why outsiders had such difficulty in studying Gypsies, and why Yoors's experience was
so valuable. He became one of the tribe, an insider.

The tribe of Gypsies that adopted him were horse
traders, but he met others who were coppersmiths, iron
workers, and entertainers. Some tribes were always stealing as they traveled through the countryside, but most
Gypsies thought this irresponsible as it made the *Gorgio*
hostile to all Gypsies. Yoors's band often took what was
needed in the way of firewood or feed for their stock, but
they were careful to keep an honest reputation as horse
traders. After all, they returned to the same trading centers
year after year. A bad reputation would have soon put
them out of business.

Although Yoors's Gypsies outwardly followed the
religious practices of their host countries, their faith had
some unique features. His friends spoke of God and the
devil, but they did not seem to believe in heaven or hell.
Although it was important to die with a clear conscience,
everyone went to the same resting place. Actually, death
was not final to the Gypsies until the last to remember a
friend or an ancestor had died. Then, when no one could
remember a person, he or she was truly dead.

The strength of the Gypsy faith rose from ancestor
worship. Much was made of Gypsy genealogy, and stories
of the old people and their exploits were often told around
the Gypsy fires. But there was no written record. In fact,
when Yoors was with his tribe in the last years of peace
before World War II, very few Gypsies knew how to read
or write. Those were things the *Caje* had to do because of
their weak memories.

Most Gypsies changed their names to suit the circum-
stances. Only close members of a family might know a

man's real name. Casual friends might know the man by one name while horse traders would use a different one. If false papers were being used to cross borders, a Gypsy might have a different name for each country of his or her travels. The *Gorgio* in a certain area might be given a name that stood for an obscenity in the Gypsy language. This, the Gypsies thought, was a good joke.

Yoors's friends were practical. They made friends with the *Gorgio* when it served a good purpose. Thus just about every major community had a Gypsy friend, often an innkeeper, who would hold mail, take phone calls, or transmit messages for the Gypsies. These *Gorgio* friends were usually willing to provide a safe stopping place for the tired travelers or even for Gypsies wanted by police.

Despite their travels, the Gypsy bands, separated by many miles, stayed in touch with one another. The *Gorgio* contacts helped, but there were other methods. When on the move, Gypsies always left signs or *patrins* to show their direction of travel. Sometimes the sign would be nothing more than a small piece of cloth tied to a branch at about wagon-seat level. It showed where the band had taken a turn or left the road. Other signs might be a few pieces of broken glass or rusty tins placed beside the remains of a small fire. Such natural looking signs not only told the direction of travel, but also told how many were in the band.

The Gypsies also drew or painted secret marks on fences or curbs in front of *Gorgio* homes to tell about the people who lived there. Such signs could warn of hostility or encourage fortune telling.

During most of the year, the tribe traveled in horse-drawn wagons. The wagons, roofed and walled with just a few windows, had large wheels that enabled them to get

These people are not friendly
to Gypsies.

A marriage is planned here.

These are Gypsy friends.

The master of this house
died recently.

You can tell fortunes here.

We robbed this place earlier.

Many Gypsies left secret signs in front of houses to tell about the occupants. These particular symbols were abandoned soon after they were published in a magazine several years ago.

over rough ground. When weather permitted, the Gypsies cooked and slept outdoors. Even when it rained, they would cook under tarps strung among the trees. During the harsh months of winter, however, the Gypsies made a permanent camp. They lived inside the drafty wagons, which were heated only by small wood stoves. It was not a comfortable time. The Gypsies began traveling again at the first signs of spring, just as soon as they could free their wagons from the grip of mud and ice.

Concentrated persecution of the Gypsies began with

the Nazi aggression. Hitler put Gypsies and Jews in the same class—people to be eliminated. The Jews could be easily rounded up and sent to the extermination camps, but the Gypsies scattered like leaves in the wind. While six million Jews were killed by the Nazis, just half-a-million Gypsies were caught and killed. Those who survived helped undermine Nazi authority wherever possible.

Many Gypsies in the underground specialized in forged documents that saved thousands from the Nazi terror. Gypsies also helped many escape from Nazi Germany. Because of their travels, the Gypsies had more "safe" contacts than the average *Gorgio*, and from previous dealings, some Gypsies knew exactly who in the underworld could be trusted and who could not.

Today, there are still Gypsies traveling in horse-drawn carts, but they are rare. Actually, most Gypsies have settled down, putting their children in schools as the law requires, and taking permanent jobs in order to enjoy a higher standard of living than before.

You can still see Gypsy fortune-tellers at county fairs. You might also see beggars and pickpockets who are genuine Gypsies. And there are Gypsies who still wander, but most prefer the automobile over the wooden wagon. In the United States, large Cadillacs are the favorite "Gypsy Wagon." In Europe, BMWs and Mercedes Benzes are preferred. And Gypsies use buses, trains, airlines. In fact, the goal of many of today's wanderers is Australia. And you can't get there in a horse-drawn wagon.

Chapter Nine

The Vikings

The young men of Norway, Sweden, and Denmark—the Vikings—had good cause to leave their homes and sail the seas seeking their fortunes. First of all, the northerners, or Norse, were much more efficient at reproducing themselves than they were in producing crops from their rockbound soil. The Viking age was an exodus from a crowded world as much as it was a conquest.

Hardly a new problem, it was undoubtedly overpopulation that had forced earlier Scandinavians to migrate into central Europe and become the Germanic tribes that played such key roles in the Age of Migration.

Through most of the seventh century, Scandinavians made a heroic effort to bring marginal land into production, but the land simply was not good enough to meet the needs of the ever-growing population. Food shortage alone can be ample cause for migration, but in Scandinavia there were other factors at work.

By 800 A.D., when Norse departures were well underway, the people followed a code of inheritance common among many early people. Known as primogeniture, the code left all property to the oldest son and nothing to younger sons and daughters. The disinherited had little choice but to seek their fortunes elsewhere.

Because some of the first Viking expeditions originated in Norway, many scholars have speculated that unusual political pressure there may also have contributed to the exodus. It is true that Harald Fine-Hair united all of Norway under his harsh rule, but this did not happen until the middle of the ninth century, well after the Viking Age had begun. Earlier efforts at political consolidation, however, may have been a factor.

Whatever their reason for taking to the sea, the Vikings had the means—wonderful boats unlike any designed or built before.

For its size and purpose, the Viking longboat cannot be improved upon even by modern designers. The boat was shallow enough to be sailed up most rivers and estuaries. When rowed, it skimmed over the water with little resistance. Yet it was broad enough to be superbly stable in a rough sea. Its broad beam also gave it great carrying capacity. The Viking cargo vessel or *knorr* could carry livestock, plows, tools, and many other necessities for colonization. Even the smaller raiding boats could carry a crew of ninety with provisions enough for extended sea voyages.

The typical Viking longboat had a high stern and bow, the stems of which were usually decorated with fierce dragon heads. There were places for as many as fifteen oars on a side. Round, brightly colored shields were lined along the railings to protect the rowers.

The longboat was probably not "invented." More

A decorative carving from a Viking picture stone shows a longboat manned with warriors who seem ready to go into battle. The shallow draft of these boats combined with their large carrying capacity made them ideal for coastal trading and raiding.

likely it was "developed" by trial and error through many generations of shipbuilders. Perhaps the Swedes, who had been profiting from Baltic trade for some four centuries prior to the Viking Age, perfected the design.

Actually, Sweden enjoyed a Golden Age of trade before the Viking Age began. Swedish princes grew rich. Cities such as Helgö on Lake Mälar, not far from present-day Stockholm, became capitals of commerce. By the start of the ninth century, Swedish traders were extending their routes far into Russia. The low country west of the Ural mountains was drained by huge rivers such as the Dvina, Dnieper, Don, and Volga. With a shallow-draft boat, it was possible to portage from the headwaters of one river to the headwaters of the next. The necessity of portage may have had a strong influence on the design of the Viking boats.

The legendary Rurik, leader of a band of Vikings or *Varangians,* as the Russians called them, was reportedly invited by Eastern Slavs to establish a trade center at Novgorod in 862. The town became a rich and powerful clearing house for Baltic trade, and the Rurik family became a noble clan that would eventually serve as one of the ruling dynasties of Russia.

That the Swedish Vikings ranged far is proven by the excavation of more than sixty thousand Arabic coins in Scandinavia. Swedish traders may have exchanged goods with Indian and Chinese merchants. In Constantinople, Swedes enlisted in the elite Varangian Guard, the Foreign Legion of the Byzantine Empire. The Vikings, calling Russia "Greater Sweden," established trade colonies at key spots along the river routes. They built warehouses and trading posts. And they posted guards along the portage roads where merchants were most vulnerable to attack by robbers. Novgorod was just one of many cities founded by Swedish Vikings.

The Norwegian Vikings were oriented westward. Their domain was to include northern England, Scotland, and the Orkney and Shetland Islands. They went on to colonize the Faroes and Iceland, the west coast of Greenland, and finally a fringe of the North American continent.

Although the Danish Vikings ventured generally southwest into England and France, it was a Norwegian freebooter who colonized the Norman or "North Men" coast of France. Rollo the Walker, legends said, was so big that no horse could carry him. After failing to take Chartres in 911, Rollo agreed to a generous treaty in which King Charles the Simple of France granted the Vikings a vast tract of rolling farm land. The soil was so rich and productive that Rollo and his men decided not to go home. Instead, they established the first Norwegian colony on the continent.

It is usually misleading, however, to separate Vikings by national origin. At the beginning of the Viking Age, Scandinavia had no national boundaries, nor were there any agreements among the Norsemen on how the world should be divided. Although Norwegian Vikings, for example, were the first to raid the English coast, it was the Danes who colonized and eventually ruled most of the island.

Early Vikings gave their loyalty to their clan or to the community of clans where they originated. They often fought each other, sometimes in blood feuds, sometimes in major battles. In England, the Anglo-Saxons were known to hire Norwegian Vikings to fight the Danish army which included Swedish mercenaries or allies.

Nationalism, however, did mature during the Viking Age. Toward the end, a spirit of nationalism became an important incentive for new conquests and new territory. By the eleventh century this spirit had blossomed into imperialism.

Knut or Canute, who became the king of Danish England at the age of eighteen, inherited the crown of Denmark when he was thirty and went on to make himself king of Norway and part of Sweden. His North Sea dominion did not last. When he died in 1035, the empire was divided among his sons. And in England, as we have seen, Edward the Confessor won the crown for the Anglo-Saxons.

The Viking reputation for bloodthirsty piracy, stereotyped by romantic fiction and films, is misleading. There were all kinds of Vikings. Some may have even been pacifists.

It is true that marauding Vikings could be merciless and wildly destructive. Their bloody raids often left towns and villages in flames. Sometimes Vikings carried off slaves and booty so regularly that the wealth of a region played out, making further raids pointless. These fierce raids, of course, drew the attention of all Europe. Everyone from peasant to king feared the Vikings. And as with the Huns, fear was a common part of Viking strategy. Fear made it easy for a small force of Norsemen simply to appear off a coast or at the mouth of a river and demand and get tribute.

Of course, it was blackmail, and tribute did not assure lasting peace. Some Viking leaders made it their practice to use the tribute collected from a region one year to finance a full-scale raid upon the same region the following year.

But tribute brought a burden of responsibility that some Vikings were willing to accept. If princes were to pay handsomely for immunity, they must be prosperous, and prosperity was possible only if farmers, craftsmen, and merchants could work in peace. For the Vikings, acceptance of responsibility was the first step toward colonialism.

The constructive nature of the Viking Age has long been underplayed. Let us look, for example, at the westward expansion.

Early histories tell us that the Shetland and Orkney Islands were added to Harald Fine-Hair's domain late in the ninth century to destroy the bases of Viking pirates who had been preying on Viking shipping. Harald, the histories say, also subdued the Hebrides and the Isle of Man. The archeological record, however, tells a different story. Relics and house foundations found at several digs suggest that Viking habitation on some of these off-shore islands dates back to late in the eighth century. And because of the lack of weapons found among the tools at

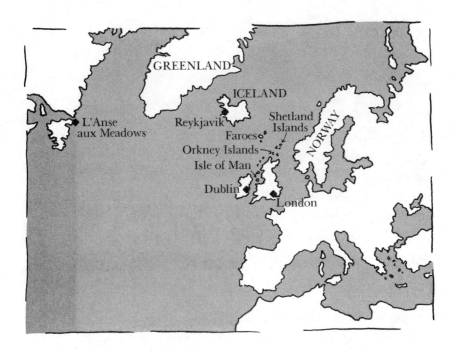

The westward migration of Vikings was achieved through a series of trade and colonizing ventures that generally had far more constructive results than the raiding voyages of Vikings to the south.

some sites, it appears that the first Viking settlers were peaceful farmers who were content to assimilate with the native Picts with little or no bloodshed.

Harald did establish dominion over the Orkneys and the Shetlands, leaving their rule to Sigurd, a prow-man on the royal longboat, who was given the title of earl. It was a prosperous domain. The islands lay close to North Sea shipping lanes, and they produced enough whale oil, fine cloth, fish, hides, and meat to play an important role in provisioning Viking expeditions and supplying Viking trade goods. A treasure horde of silver found on the main island of the Orkneys contained ninety separate pieces and weighed a total of sixteen pounds. Graves rich in jewels and ornaments have also been unearthed.

For many years, the Scottish mainland was ruled by the Orkney earldom, and although Viking rule in England ended in 1066, it continued in Scotland for another hundred years. By then, the Vikings of the north islands had been following the Christian faith for many generations.

The Isle of Man, a 227-square-mile patch of earth in the middle of the Irish Sea, was colonized about halfway through the ninth century by Norwegian Vikings who again seem to have come in peace. The Vikings, influenced by the Christianity taught by the native Celts, adopted the new faith but retained belief in many of the old gods. Viking burial crosses were decorated with figures of the Norse god Odin being devoured by the wolf Fanir. For Norsemen, the scene was symbolic of life's last battle. Weapons and other treasures continued to be buried in Christian graves. In one grave, a wife or slave girl, killed by a blow on the head, was buried on top of a dead Viking.

Although evidence of human sacrifice has been found in Scandinavia and in Viking graves in Russia, the Isle of Man grave provides the only known evidence of the pagan ritual in the British Isles.

Rulers of Man were appointed by the Norwegian king, but the island enjoyed a great deal of independent government with a democratic bent. Many decisions were made by the Tynwald or assembly of chiefs which met every summer to adopt laws and administer justice. A ceremonial meeting of the Tynwald is still held on July 5 of every year. Viking control ended, however, in 1266, when Magnus, the last king of the island, agreed to accept Scottish rule.

The history of the Vikings in Ireland is clouded by biased writing. The early chroniclers, wanting to glorify the Celtic defenders, describe the invaders as cruel beasts who killed monks and plundered monasteries and wasted the land wherever they went. Actually, the Irish themselves had been robbing the rich monasteries long before the first Viking was first reported in 795.

By then, Ireland was the leading Christian state in the post-Roman world. Its missionaries traveled everywhere. Its churches and monasteries had amassed fortunes in precious metals and jewels as well as livestock and full graneries. In time of famine, Irish peasants attacked the monasteries simply to get life's necessities. Bands of monks and followers from rival monasteries even attacked each other.

When the first Vikings arrived, some Celts might even have joined them and led the way to the monasteries. In any case the Vikings continued to raid Irish settlements for almost two generations before starting to establish colonies. The first attempt at colonization is credited to Turgesius, a legendary Norwegian sea king, who reportedly plundered Armagh Abbey and then used it as a palace from which he tried to convert all Ireland to paganism. The story does not fit the Viking character. Most Norsemen did not believe in their gods with enough zeal to impose the faith on anyone else. Actually scholars are not sure today if Turgesius ever existed, but archeologists have unearthed evidence of Viking communities that date back to about 840 A.D.

The most interesting discoveries from the colonial sites are the tools, including forge pincers and tongs, hammers, shears, sickles, and knives that were buried with the craftsmen who used them. These things, along with balance scales and weights, were probably unknown in Ireland prior to the arrival of the Vikings. Scholars thus believe that the Vikings introduced several crafts as well as trade. And with the start of Viking colonization, the Irish replaced their crude hide-covered boats or *currachs*

Typical daub-and-wattle house construction called for many wattles or willow-like limbs woven between upright posts that were firmly anchored in the ground. The woven framework was later daubed with mud to make an airtight wall.

with sleek longboats. The Irish also adopted some of the Norse trade vocabulary. Words such as "market" and "penny" can be traced to the Viking *margad* and *peningr*.

Vikings never attempted to control Ireland politically, but by holding monopolies on wine, textiles and other important trade goods, they gained economic control as well as great personal wealth and power. Actually, it seems that the Vikings tried to avoid the politics of the day. The Celtic chiefs, trying to expand their territories, were constantly fighting each other. Occasionally, when it seemed to their advantage, the Vikings took sides in these disputes, but usually they fought only to keep their ports open.

Dublin, the largest port, was founded by Vikings. Archeological digs in the heart of the modern city, one on High Street and the other on Winetavern Street, have unearthed the remains of Viking streets, wooden sidewalks, and houses and shops built in the post-and-wattle style. The walls of such houses were made by weaving long whips of willow or other branches horizontally between posts set upright in the ground.

The rubbish heaps showed that the Vikings enjoyed a varied diet: pork, mutton, and beef; snipe, woodcock, and other game birds; oysters, mussels, clams, and scallops; strawberries, apples, plums, and cherries; and wheat and barley. Such foodstuffs, along with local wines, were used in Viking trade as were the products of Viking Dublin's many shops.

Archeologists discovered a bone carver's shop that specialized in pocket combs. It also produced knife handles, bone whistles, and ornamental game pieces for chess-like games. Another shop produced wooden bowls and plates, some of which were turned on a hand-powered lathe. This shop contained the carved model of a Viking longboat.

Cobblers' shops were making shoes with methods that were to remain unchanged for four hundred years and more. In a metalworking shop, archeologists found clay pots for smelting bronze and casting molds carved from soapstone. A popular casting was a small hammer to be worn around the neck for good luck. This represented the hammer of Thor, the Norse god who pounded out thunder and lightning from his heavenly forge.

Although Dublin remained the commercial capital of Ireland, other Viking trade centers such as Waterford, Wicklow, Wexford, and Limerick did a prosperous business. There was good profit in weapons and other supplies for the wars that were almost endless among the Irish chiefs. Although the Vikings were happy to let the Irish do most of the fighting, Vikings did eventually get entangled in revolt. It happened early in the eleventh century when Brian Boru, the king of Munster, won enough battles to call himself king of Ireland. Of course, his claim was challenged. He had to keep fighting.

His final battle was fought at Clontarf, near Dublin, in 1014. There, according to legend, Brian Boru gave his life to break the Viking power in his country. Actually, the Irish chieftain was trying to suppress a revolt raised by

*This coin, found in Dublin, was one
of many minted by the Vikings
to promote trade with England and
mainland Europe. Before the Vikings,
little Irish trade was attempted.*

Leinster, which had hired Norse mercenaries from the Orkneys and the Isle of Man as well as from the local trade ports.

Although Boru was killed in the battle, his army routed the rebels and their Vikings. But contrary to legend, the Vikings were not driven from Ireland. They continued to dominate Irish commerce for more than a century. It was not until 1160, when Dermot MacMurrough Kavanagh, another in a long line of defeated Irish chiefs, asked England for help, that the Normans sent an army that squashed all resistance, drove the Vikings away, and put the Irish under British rule.

Judging from recent history, the Irish might have been happier had they kept the Vikings.

For many Norsemen, Ireland was just a stepping stone in westward expansion across the Atlantic. Two hundred miles to the northwest, the bleak Faroes provided another stepping stone. When the first Vikings arrived in about 800 A.D., they found the islands sparsely populated by Irish monks. The monks reportedly fled in their skin boats, leaving behind the sheep that they had introduced on the island some fifty years earlier.

The new settlers were farmers who built their colony on sheep raising, fishing, and egg gathering from the many wild bird rookeries. And they produced woolens for trade. Life was not easy. The steep cliffs made boat landings difficult, and the weather was bleak. But, the little colony prospered, providing the base for further exploration.

Vikings discovered Iceland by accident about the middle of the ninth century. Probably traders bound for the Orkneys were blown off course, sighted the island, and returned to Norway with the news. Timing was ripe for colonization. By now, political pressure as well as land shortage were indeed sparking the migratory urge. Harald Fine-Hair had most of Norway under his ruthless authority.

Those who had resisted his tyranny were wanted men. The first expedition of colonials to reach Iceland was led by Ingølf Arnarson who had offended one of Harald's chieftains. Before sailing, Arnarson, a pagan and a slave owner, made sacrifice, perhap human sacrifice, to the gods. And when off the east coast of Iceland, uncertain where to settle, he gave way to further superstition. According to the Iceland Sagas, which recorded both the legend and history of Iceland and its people, Ingølf took the wooden pillars from a large chair, apparently a family throne of honor, and threw them overboard. Wherever they drifted ashore, Ingølf vowed, there would he build his home.

The Vikings reportedly wandered across the 39,700-square-mile island for three years before finding the chair pillars cast up on the shore of a beautiful bay on the western shore. The bay was embraced by blue mountains, and steam plumes from many hot springs rose in the crisp air. There, in 874, the early accounts say, the colonists built homes with thick walls of turf and stone and began farming. The spot was not far from Reykjavik, modern capital of the Icelandic Republic.

The Vikings were not the first to inhabit the island. Like the Faroes, it had been sparsely settled by Irish monks who fled when the Norsemen appeared. Actually, discovery may date back to Roman times. A recent find of copper coins dating from the third-century A.D. Rome suggests that Iceland may have been the *Ultima Thule* mentioned by ancient geographers.

The Vikings, however, were the first colonists. They came with a rush. By 930 A.D. barely sixty years after the first landing, there were some ten thousand Vikings and their slaves living on Iceland. They were a mixed lot. While many came from western and southern Norway, the Norse colonies on the Orkneys, the Shetlands, and Ireland were well represented. Some were pagans. Many others were Christians. Among the latter were some with Celtic blood and Celtic culture.

Although they differed in many ways, all Icelanders wanted to govern themselves, independent of Norway, and free from the tyranny of any single leader. They laid the seed of their republic with an annual meeting of chieftains. The Althing, as it is called, first met in 930 and has been described as Europe's oldest parliament.

The chieftains elected a president, or "Law-Speaker," who was charged with memorizing every law ever adopted by the Althing. Whoever held the office of president had to recite the laws annually. This custom continued until the laws were finally written down in 1119 A.D.

Iceland long remained
part Christian and part pagan.
This bronze statue is of Thor,
the Norse god of thunder.

The Althing had its defects. For one thing, it gave the chieftains too much power. Some, knowing they could gain the support of their fellow chiefs, took the law in their own hands, even to the extremity of killing their enemies. There was no police force and no executive to enforce rulings or carry out orders. Civil judgments meant little if the winning side did not have the power to collect what was awarded it.

But the Althing embodied the spirit of democracy, and it did solve some difficult problems. The most difficult arose in 1000 A.D., when Olaf Tryggvason, then king of Norway, demanded that Iceland, along with other colonies, adopt Christianity as its official and only religion. Olaf's order drew the battle line between pagans and Christians. They had been living in peace on Iceland, but suddenly the two sides seemed ready for battle. The pagans, of course, won supporters by citing Olaf's order as tampering with Icelandic independence, but the Christians had a stronger commitment to their faith than the pagans.

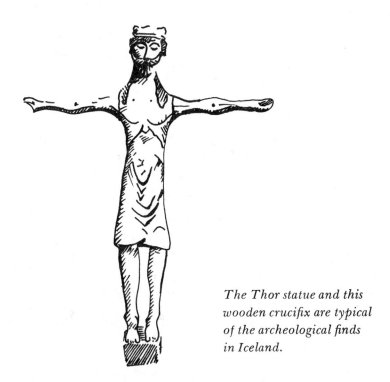

*The Thor statue and this
wooden crucifix are typical
of the archeological finds
in Iceland.*

The Althing, meeting to debate the issue, asked the
Law-Speaker to decide which faith Iceland should adopt.
The Law-Speaker, himself a pagan, retired for twenty hours
before coming forth with his verdict. Iceland, he said,
should become a Christian country, but pagans could go
on practicing their beliefs as long as they did not offend
anyone.

The compromise was not only accepted, but it also
worked. If other nations had been as wise, a great deal of
bloody history might have been avoided.

In criminal matters, the Althing's most common sentence was banishment. This led to further Norse migration.

In about 981, Eric the Red, who had killed some other
Icelanders in a blood feud, was banished from the island
for three years. Eric was both practical and philosophical
about the sentence. His father, after all, had brought his
family to Iceland as a fugitive from Harald Fine-Hair's
oppression, and the family had prospered. Eric decided
to spend his banishment in exploration.

Greenland, some 160 miles to the northwest, had already been discovered by wandering Vikings. In fact, there had been an early effort at colonizing the inhospitable east coast of the large island. That effort had failed. Eric decided to explore the south and west coasts of Greenland.

He sailed in about 982. He and his fellow Vikings found good fishing and hunting and many sheltered coves, but best of all they found land that could be farmed. When he returned to Iceland after his banishment, Eric promoted a new effort at colonization. To make it sound attractive, and perhaps knowing that the name "Iceland," had tended to discourage settlement, Eric called the new country Greenland.

A fleet of twenty-five ships sailed. A storm scattered them, but fourteen ships arrived safely in a cove just beyond the southern tip of Greenland, not far from the present day Julianehaab. Other colonists followed, establishing farmsteads farther and farther north along the island's west coast. Independent rule based on an Althing much like Iceland's was established. The colony thrived. The population was to grow steadily until the twelfth century when it reached a peak of ten thousand.

By then, some Greenlanders had tried to establish colonies on North America. The Iceland Sagas give two conflicting accounts of the Viking discovery of the New World.

One account from *Eric's Saga,* says that Eric's son, Leif, returning from Norway in 999 A.D. to bring Christianity to Greenland, was blown off course so that "he came upon lands whose existence he never expected." After arriving in Greenland and converting the colonists to Christianity, he set sail to explore the new lands.

In the *Greenlendinga Saga,* Bjarni Herjølfsson, another storm-driven sailor, is credited with discovering America. Bjarni, however, was not interested in exploration, and when he arrived in Greenland, he sold his boat to Leif who set sail in about 990 with a crew of thirty-five.

The saga goes on to say that Leif and his men first landed on barren, rocky country, probably Baffin Island directly west of Greenland, and then sailed south. They passed a forested coast, probably Newfoundland, and after two more days sailing, made another landfall. Here they came ashore. They found the country rich in grassy pasture, and "there was no lack of salmon in the river."

Leif and his men decided to spend the winter. They built some large houses and explored the countryside. On one expedition, the crewman Tyrkir found some wild grapes. Leif thus christened the land Vinland or Wineland. They returned to Greenland the following spring with a cargo of lumber and dried grapes. On the way they rescued the passengers and crew of a shipwreck from a small island. Among those saved was Gudrid, a woman who was to have an important role in the sagas.

In Greenland, she married Thorfinn Karlsefni, and together they led an expedition back to Vinland. According to *Eric's Saga,* there were three boats with one hundred sixty people intent on colonization. The venture lasted three years. In Vinland, the native Americans were apparently willing to trade peacefully with the colonists. But some Norsemen cheated them. The natives became hostile, and even though their weapons were inferior, they outnumbered the colonists.

While under threat of native attack Gudrid gave birth to a son. Snorri Thorfinnsson, as he was called, was the first white child to be born in the New World. He was not to stay for the colonists realized they could not hold out against the natives.

After loading their ships with rich cargo, Thorfinn and Gudrid led the expedition back to Greenland. Vinland was soon forgotten.

Today, no one is sure where it is.

Archeologists have excavated sites along the coast of the continent and found remains of several Norse settlements or encampments. One site, L'Anse aux Meadows at the north tip of Newfoundland, included the remains of old buildings, but no certain evidence of Leif Ericsson's Vinland has yet been found. But for most scholars, the sagas are proof enough that the Vikings discovered America five centuries before Christopher Columbus set sail.

By the time of Columbus, however, the Greenland colony had mysteriously vanished. Where had ten thousand Vikings gone? There are many theories. One has it that a change to colder climate made profitable farming impossible. Another theory holds that the Norsemen, who referred to the native Eskimos as *Skraelings* or Wretches, paid for their prejudice by being wiped out or driven away by Eskimo raids. Still another theory has it that the colonists were assimilated into the Eskimo tribes.

Whatever the cause, we do know that Norway, which added Greenland to its domain in the thirteenth century, neglected the colony for more than two centuries. When English sailors rediscovered Greenland in the sixteenth century, no Norsemen could be found.

Chapter Ten

Genghis Khan

Proud, independent, fierce, and resourceful, the Mongols of the bleak Gobi Desert acknowledged but one master—hunger. In late winter, when the hunters returned with no meat and the herds could find no grass on the snow-blown slopes, hunger became a cruel ruler. Mongols went for days without food. Always at these times there were some who starved to death.

The people could eat anything. Mare's milk was an important food, but when there was no milk, hungry Mongols often cut a horse's vein and drank warm blood as it flowed. A Mongol counted his wealth by the number of horses and cattle in his herds. But such wealth was never permanent.

Raids among the clans were common. A small band on swift horses could drive away a neighbor's herds and escape before an alarm could be given. Sometimes the raiders burned the felt tents of a neighboring clan and galloped off with booty. Food sacks were the main prize,

When they weren't tending their herds of animals or hunting, Mongols spent much time and energy fighting each other. Here two horsemen with their quivers full of arrows look for battle with a neighboring tribe.

but anything else of value, including women, slaves, or weapons might also be taken.

For the proud Mongols, raids and any other wrong done the clan or the family had to be avenged. Blood feuds were accepted as a necessary part of Mongol life. It was also necessary to keep moving. As the herds grazed the slopes bare, scouts rode out to find new grass.

With few possessions, the Mongols moved with ease. The men rounded up the animals. The women rolled up the tents and loaded them and the tent poles onto the ox carts. Some spare clothing, perhaps a chest or two of silks and jewelry, also went on the carts. Then the move began, the carts following the dusty trail of the herds.

It was almost impossible to unite such people under a single ruler. True, the ancestors of these people had united and as the Huns had forced the Chinese to start building their Great Wall as early as the third century B.C. Then, as we have seen, the Huns began the western drive that changed the map of Europe. But since the Hun migration, the people living in and around the Gobi Desert had not been united.

The most desirable part of the Mongol territory lay
east of Lake Baykal. Here, high mountains took some bite
from the cold winds, and the many rivers, including the
Kerulon to the north and the Onon to the south, flowed
down from the mountains, watering the pastureland to
produce some of the best grass in the entire region. For
many centuries various tribes battled fiercely to control
this rich region. Control passed from one tribe to another,
but in the twelfth century A.D. it was held by the Yakka.

This tribe had prospered under the protection of
Yesukai, a strong chieftain who had the loyalty and respect
of most clans of the tribe. At one time Yesukai's domain
was numbered at forty thousand Yakka tents. As a fighter,
Yesukai was valiant and clever. He led his mounted warriors on frequent raids or reprisals that kept most of his
enemies at bay.

But Yesukai's domain was never secure. He knew
that if he stopped raiding border tribes, his people would
start fighting among themselves. Then all he had worked
to build would be lost.

He had many enemies, this Yesukai. In one raid, he
attacked tents where a wedding was taking place. Yesukai
rode away with the bride and kept her for his own. Such
a deed was an insult that even the Yakka agreed must one
day be avenged. But the bride, Houlun, once her grief
passed, bore Yesukai several sons. The first of them was a
red-haired boy called Temujin.

Once weaned, Mongol children had to fend for themselves. They hunted and fished to stay alive. In the tents,
they had to crawl and wriggle between the adults to find
warmth from the winter fire.

Temujin had a temper to match his red hair. One of
the first stories about him tells that when a half-brother

stole a fish from him, Temujin killed the boy in a rage of temper. Yesukai may have scolded him for this, but among the Mongols, theft from a friend or relative was often punished by death. According to Mongol code, Temujin had done the correct thing.

The boy learned early that the loyalty of a friend was one of life's most valued possessions. And Temujin also discovered early that loss of loyalty could be devastating.

When he was just thirteen, Temujin's father died of poison given him while visiting an enemy tent. Before their chief's body was cold, the Yakka began to scatter.

Although Temujin was heir to all his father owned, few tribesmen would trust their safety to a thirteen-year-old boy. The herdsmen wanted a leader who was older, more experienced, and stronger.

Houlun, Temujin's mother, was soon alone, protected only by a few friends and her sons. Everyone knew that Yesukai's enemies would now try to take revenge on Temujin, her firstborn.

After urging the family to flee, the few remaining friends began to drift away. But Houlun refused to run. Temujin himself was determined to secure his birthright.

It was a desperate struggle. Bowmen on swift horses hunted the family. Houlun and her sons escaped again and again. But no one could be trusted. Finally, Temujin was captured and yoked so that his hands were bound helplessly to a branch tied across the back of his neck.

At night, however, he worked free from his bonds and fled. His enemies pursued him. He hid in a river among some concealing reeds. He remained in the cold water for many hours. Later, when it was safe to leave his hiding place, he persuaded a merchant to hide him in a cartload of wool.

Such adventures, recounted among the clans, gradually built Temujin's reputation as a quick-witted and courageous lad.

When he wasn't tricking and eluding his enemies, Temujin visited once-loyal clansmen, reminding them of his birthright, trying to rebuild the tribe. But the wary Mongols held back. Even though the boy had proved clever and daring, he was still a boy.

Temujin was often discouraged, but the worst setback came when he returned to his mother's tent one day to hear that the family's horses had been stolen. Eight were gone, leaving just one old horse to ride in pursuit of the thieves.

At once, Temujin began tracking the herd. He never would have caught the thieves, however, if he had not met a stranger who not only agreed to lend him a fresh horse but also offered to go with him. Together, the two found the thieves' camp and in the dark of night recovered the stolen horses. In their escape, the new friend, whose name was Borchu, used his bow to kill one of the thieves who was chasing them.

Borchu, of course, had already heard the stories about the young chieftain. Now that he had shared an adventure with him, he was determined to devote the rest of his life to serving Temujin. Temujin had this effect on people.

Other strong friendships were formed during his years as a fugitive. Temujin always rewarded those who helped him. He tried to give Borchu half the horses that had been recovered, but Borchu refused, saying Temujin's friendship was reward enough.

Temujin's growing group of friends praised him as a

hero who had earned the tribe's loyalty. Gradually, the Yakka chiefs returned. After all, the boy had not fled from the home pastureland. And he was older now, more experienced. With help, he might keep the land between the rivers safe from enemy tribes.

His confidence growing, Temujin went to the tent of Bourtai, a young girl who had been betrothed to him years earlier. After three days of feasting, dancing, and much drinking of rice wine and fermented mare's milk, the two were married. Temujin was seventeen. His bride was thirteen.

The young pair barely had time to set up and furnish their own tent when disaster struck unexpectedly.

Fierce tribesmen from the north, men of the tundra who used reindeer and dogs to draw their sleds, attacked the Yakka. Temujin was able to mount a horse and shoot enough arrows to clear a path of escape, but Bourtai was captured. Some accounts say that these northern raiders were avenging Yesukai's kidnapping of Houlun years before. If so, the raiders did not enjoy their success for long.

Temujin, getting help from the Karaits, a tribe to the south that had long been friends of the Yakka, rode after the raiders. He led a moonlight attack on their camp, calling Bourtai's name until she rushed from the ruins of a tent. He swung her into his saddle, called off the attack, and galloped into the night. He had recovered what was his.

Actually, the northern tribes did not threaten the Mongols as much as those to the east. They attacked constantly.

During one bloody campaign, Temujin fell with an arrow in his throat. His comrades sucked the blood from his wound and washed it with melted snow. They stole food from an enemy camp to nourish their leader. During a blizzard, they took turns holding a cloak over Temujin to shelter him from the cold.

After a long sleep, the lad recovered enough strength to ride home. As Bourtai nursed him back to health, he made sure that those who saved him were well rewarded. The tradition of loyalty was building.

Another crisis came during the annual move from the high summer pastures down to the valleys. Though Temujin now had thirteen thousand warriors in his command, they were strung out on the trail with their tent carts and their herds. It was a dangerous time, and the Yakka's eastern enemies took advantage of it. The attacking horde came over the horizon thirty thousand strong.

To flee would mean the loss of the women and the cattle. Temujin did not even consider this, nor did he risk an attack. His early years had taught him to be resourceful, and he did something completely new to Mongol tactics. After ordering the carts into a defensive square, he put the women and children inside the carts and then drove the cattle inside the enclosure.

As his warriors gathered he formed them up so that one end of his line was protected by a forest and the other end was protected by the square of wagons. In this way, Temujin was able to present a narrow, but strong front to the enemy.

The enemy attack began with a charge of light cavalry. Though swift, the horses and men wore no armor. Temujin's bowmen were superb marksmen. They turned the attackers back with just a few volleys of deadly arrows. Next the enemy charged with armed cavalry. The riders wore helmets of hard leather and steel plates lashed to their chests with thongs. Their horses were protected with leather thick enough to stop most arrows. Temujin led his own heavy cavalry against the charge.

Though they were outnumbered, the Yakka horsemen had the advantage of a narrow front. They concentrated a fierce attack on one section of the enemy line, breaking it and throwing the rest of the horde into confusion. Temujin's warriors loosed their arrows, felling enemy horsemen by the thousands.

At the end of the day, five to six thousand of the enemy lay dead. Seventy chieftains had been captured. Temujin had brought victory from what seemed certain defeat. Was there ever such a leader of men?

Now Temujin believed he had enough loyal followers, enough power to seek alliance with other tribes. He went to Toghrul, leader of the Karaits who had helped him recapture Bourtai.

The Karaits, more settled than the Mongols, had permanent towns and villages. Some of them were farmers, and their territory was crossed by roads that linked the lands of Islam to the west with China to the east. Many Karaits were traders, and some, through contact with Christians, had adopted that religion.

Toghrul himself was probably not a Christian, but stories about him gave rise to the legendary Prester John whom most Europeans of the time believed ruled the East with justice and Christian benevolence.

Toghrul not only agreed to an alliance with the Mongols, but he was also willing to adopt Temujin as his son, establishing a symbolic kinship between their two tribes. The first achievement of the union was to break the strength of the eastern clans. The action extended the Mongol territory to the Great Wall that marked the frontier to China, which was then known as Cathay.

No one was surprised when Temujin, shown here in a drawing made from a contemporary portrait, was elected "Emperor of All Men."

The victory over the eastern tribes upset a delicate balance of power in the Gobi. Turkish tribes to the west, old enemies of the Mongols, now feared the Mongols, lacking any other enemies, could attack them. Leaders of the Turkish tribes went to Toghrul and somehow persuaded the aging ruler to break his alliance with Temujin and join them in attacking the Mongols.

The first battle raged all day at the mouth of a desert

gorge. At the beginning, the Mongols held their ground, but their losses were so heavy that they eventually had to withdraw. Although Temujin had lost an important fight, he saved his army.

He held a council of chieftains. They spent most of the winter planning their campaign. Early in the spring, Mongol warriors were the first in the field. They surprised the main Karait camp. Toghrul fled for his life only to be killed by the same Turks who had earlier persuaded him to break the Mongol treaty.

Meanwhile, Temujin held the main body of the Karait army surrounded. He promised to spare those who would join him, and the Karait warriors, most of whom had lost faith in their leaders, joined the Mongols by the thousands.

Now master of the Gobi, Temujin did not pause to celebrate victory. Instead, he led his warriors against the Turkish tribes, subduing them one by one. He killed their leaders, distributed the women among his warriors, and sent captive warriors to live among dependable allies. In this manner his empire and his fame grew. It was an honor to serve such a wise and courageous leader, a man who kept his word and could treat even his enemies fairly.

Complete defeat of the Turkish tribes took just three years. When the last campaign ended, Temujin called another council of chieftains. He told them that they must select a man to rule the empire. To no one's surprise, Temujin was named "Emperor of All Men" or Genghis Kha Khan.

Chapter Eleven

The Mongol Conquest

At this point, most ordinary rulers might have been tempted to relax and enjoy the benefits of empire, but Genghis Khan was far from ordinary. Neither were his people. The Mongols, though nomads and often cruel in battle, were not savages. They had unwritten customs that governed conduct much like the westerners' Ten Commandments.

Genghis Khan, who recognized the great advantage of a written language in government, collected a staff of scribes from among his captives and taught them to write and interpret for himself and his officers. A formal code of conduct was one of the first things the khan had written down.

The Mongol Code or Yassa required that false witnesses, spies, and thieves be put to death. It also said that children must respect their parents, that a man must respect his leaders, and that a rich man must help the poor.

The main purposes of the code were to assure absolute loyalty to the khan, to bind the clan together, and to punish wrongs. But there were some unusual features. The code said a man could get drunk only three times a month, although it would be better not to get drunk at all. The code also said Mongols should not touch water during a thunderstorm. So great was the Mongol fear of thunder and lightning that they often tried to hide from it in lakes or rivers. Genghis Khan must have realized that water was a good conductor and gave the least safety during an electrical storm.

But perhaps the most puzzling aspect of the khan's code was its first law:

"It is ordered that all men should believe in one god, creator of heaven and earth, the sole giver of goods and poverty, of life and death as pleases him, whose power over all things is absolute."

Although the Mongols may have been influenced by early Christians who preached of one god, the nomads, like native Americans, drew most of their religious beliefs from shamans or witch doctors, who invoked many deities. Genghis Khan himself was known to be tolerant of and curious about all religions. So why did he demand worship of a single god?

Could it be that when he spoke of "god" he was referring to himself? Many Mongols believed he was a god. In fact, it was a tradition to believe that strong rulers had divine powers. Possibly the khan believed it himself.

Although we cannot say exactly what religious faith Genghis Khan followed, we can be certain of one rule of government that dominated his entire career. He knew he must keep his Mongols at war. If they ever stopped fighting an enemy they would soon be fighting among themselves.

This was probably the main reason for the Mongols' next phase of conquest. The enemy was China. The year was 1211. Genghis Khan was thirty-four years old.

For years the Mongols had been humiliated by the powerful Chinese who required all nomads beyond the Great Wall to pay yearly tribute to their Golden Emperor. But the Chin dynasty, though it ruled northern China, had long been at war with the house of Sung which ruled southern China. And in northern China itself there were tribes along the northern frontier who were ready to revolt.

The Chinese army, however, could not be taken lightly. Officers began their careers by studying the art of war in formal military schools. Soldiers were well equipped and well trained. And there was an endless supply of manpower.

Genghis Khan, well aware of the risk, had already sent some of his warriors to the south to fight on the side of the Sung. They learned what the country was like and gained a full understanding of fighting tactics. Thus when news arrived that the old Chin emperor was dead and had been replaced on the throne by his young son, Wai Wang, Genghis Khan decided the time had come. He stopped paying tribute to the new emperor.

The Chinese attacked first by sending units beyond the wall to punish the Mongols. Genghis Khan countered with all his warriors. The Chinese fled before the horde.

Mongol scouts, riding in pairs, led the way. They were followed by an advance force of thirty thousand choice horsemen. Then came a line of three armies of one hundred thousand riders each. Genghis Khan led the central force.

He had prepared well. Spies had already gone into enemy territory, paying bribes and recruiting informers and agents. Thus, when the Mongols crossed the Onon River and arrived at the Great Wall, they found the gates open for them. Genghis Khan led his army into China without losing a man.

Though the Chinese had more soldiers, their army was divided. Many units fought in the south. Others were needed in the north if the revolt there were to be put down. But even when the defenders could march in great numbers against the khan, they were no match for his fast-riding horsemen.

Wherever they went, the Mongols controlled the countryside and the small villages. The Chinese retreated behind the walls of their large cities. Merchants and nobles were forced to remain in the cities throughout the summer months. It was safe to come out only in the winter, after the khan had taken his horde back to the Gobi Desert. When spring returned, so did the Mongols.

This pattern continued for four years, and for the most part, Genghis Khan was content with it. His men were steadily winning the loyalty of the Chinese peasants. The city dwellers, who depended on the countryside for their food, would eventually be forced to make peace. There were few major battles, but sometimes the Mongols took a city by trickery.

A favorite Mongol trick was to begin a siege and then fake a sudden withdrawal. The Mongols would leave their loaded baggage carts in plain view of the enemy. The temptation was too great. In just a few hours, the Chinese would rush out through the city gates to raid the Mongol

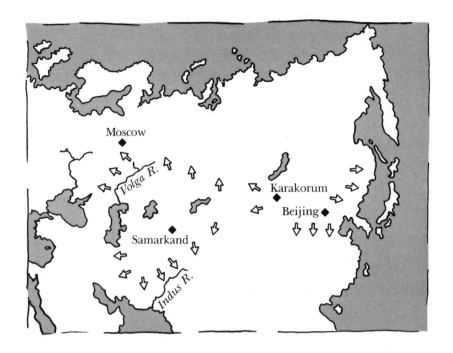

The greatest land empire the world had ever known was created by Genghis Khan. His domain stretched from the Sea of Japan to beyond the Volga River on the west and to the banks of the Indus River on the south.

supplies. When the looting was at its height, the Mongol horsemen, who had been hiding over the horizon or in a forest, would attack in force. In a few terrible moments of slaughter, the Mongols won easy entry to the city.

But the Chinese capital of Ken-king, near the site of modern Beijing, could not be taken by trickery. In fact, its walls were so strong and its defenders so well trained that it might not have fallen at all if Wai Wang had been a forceful leader. But this was not the case. In 1215, the Golden Emperor fled from the capital city, seeking safety with the Sung, his southern enemy.

His departure shattered morale. Although loyal leaders remained to defend the city, most soldiers were reluctant to die for an emperor who had given up. Many deserted. In fact, it was a relatively small band of Mongols that led a large army of deserters into the capital.

With the fall of Ken-king, Genghis Khan annexed China to his empire. News of the khan's victory shook the world. For many it was bad news, particularly for the people of Islam.

At the time of China's fall, the Islamic world seemed invincible. The khan knew vaguely of the vast realm to the west. Perhaps he had long coveted its wealth, but Islam lay on the far side of high mountains.

Only a few hardy merchants led their caravans through the high, snowy passes to trade with Cathay. From these merchants, Genghis had learned of the mighty shah of Kharesm whose domain stretched from the Indus River to the Caspian Sea and from the shores of the Arabian Gulf well into what is now southern Russia. His army was huge. His warriors were fierce and loyal. Perhaps he was almost as great as Genghis Khan himself.

The khan may have been acting out of curiosity when he sent envoys to the shah. They carried bars of silver, jade, robes of white camel hair, and other valuable gifts. And they presented a message from the khan, suggesting a trade treaty. Although it's hard to think of Genghis Khan as fostering peaceful trade, his offer to the shah was probably sincere. The land seemed too remote and the barrier mountains too high to consider war with Islam.

Indeed Mongol and Islam merchants did trade peacefully for a few years, but then the shah made a mistake. A caravan of Mongol merchants was stopped at the frontier by a suspicious governor who reported that there were spies among the merchants. On receiving this report, the shah ordered that all the merchants be killed.

Immediately, the khan sent envoys protesting this outrage. When the Mongols arrived, the shah had the leading envoy beheaded and had the beards burned from the faces of the others. It was one of history's most tragic insults.

Under the Mongol code, there was but one answer to the shah. In a brief message Genghis Khan said:

"You have chosen war. That will happen which will happen, and what it is to be, we know not. God alone knows."

To his own ministers he said there could not be two suns in heaven or two kha khans on the face of the earth.

The campaign began in 1218. It lasted six years. It annexed what are now Iran and Afghanistan and it extended Mongol influence into Southern Russia, Iraq, and India. It created the greatest land empire the world had yet known.

Many Mongol warriors who rode west across the great mountains never returned to the Gobi again. All fought as if they expected no return. They were crueler, fiercer, and more relentless than they had ever been before. When the frontier governor who killed the Mongol merchants was captured, Genghis Khan ordered molten silver poured in the man's eyes and throat.

The shah may have been a good general, but he panicked. He divided his forces, abandoned the fortress city of Bokhara, and fled with the vain hope of reuniting the army he had just divided so that he could return and repulse the Mongols. It never happened. Many of his soldiers, once so well disciplined, also lost their nerve. The Mongols soon caught up with the fleeing army and cut it to pieces.

In Bokhara, meanwhile, other Mongols looted the

granaries, collected all the treasure they could find and then burned the city to the ground. Captives were marched toward Samarkand. These prisoners were forced to help put the ancient trade center under siege.

The fleeing shah had stopped for a time at Samarkand. The city had strong defenses and a full garrison. The shah might have been able to hold out there long enough for his army to regroup, but as the Mongols approached, he abandoned his soldiers to their fate and fled again. The khan used his main army to take the city, but he sent his fastest cavalry units on the trail of the shah.

The chase led west into Iraq and then north to the shores of the Caspian Sea. Now with just a few loyal followers, the shah disguised himself and hid on an island. Later he used a fishing village on the west shore of the Caspian for his hideout, but he was betrayed by one of his own people. He was forced to return to the island, where alone and weak from disease and exhaustion, he died.

Even if Genghis Khan had heard at once of the shah's death, it is not likely that the Mongols would have retired. Their fury had been unleashed. Nothing would tame that fury.

Mongol raiders crossed the Ural River and went all the way to the Dnieper River where it flows into the Black Sea. On their return they scattered native Bulgar settlements along the Volga. Other Mongol forces pressed southward. At first the Mongols took captives from one city to help with the siege of the next, but captives slowed the Mongol attack. The policy was changed. All must be killed.

Genghis Khan said he would punish any of his men who failed to carry out this order.

Cities that resisted the Mongols were destroyed, completely. Captives were lined up and beheaded in a bloody harvest. So many bodies lay rotting in the ruins of some cities that roads had to be rerouted around them because of the stench. Eventually the ruins themselves were plowed over and planted, leaving no trace of once-proud cities.

The Moslems tried to defend their territory. The strongest resistance was organized by Jelal ed-Din, a prince of Kharesm who fielded an army of thirty thousand men. Allied for a time with an Afghani army, Jelal ed-Din gave an advance force of Mongols a sound beating. But the Afhgani alliance ended in argument, and Jelal ed-Din was soon forced to retreat. He took his final stand on the banks of the Indus River where he almost defeated Genghis Khan.

The prince's army was protected on one side by the swift river and on the other by some rugged mountains. Soon after stopping the Mongols' first advance, the prince's forces attacked from their well-protected flanks. The left side of the Mongol line was thrown back, but with their usual discipline, the horsemen regrouped and checked any further Moslem gains.

As the day wore on without any decisive developments, the prince took a big gamble. He concentrated his forces on the center of the Mongol line. He hoped to capture the khan, and he almost did. But the khan's horse was killed as the attack began, forcing him to pull back momentarily for a fresh mount. Thus, he was not there when the prince's horsemen cut their way through the line.

Instead, the khan was able to lead his own heavy cavalry in a flanking attack. Meanwhile, the Mongol center again regrouped and stopped the Moslem charge. The prince turned back to find his flank crumbling under the khan's attack.

Seeing that his army was doomed, the prince galloped to the Indus. Horse and rider plunged twenty feet into the water. The prince swam his horse to the far bank and vanished in the forest.

Genghis Khan sent a pursuit force into India. They returned without the prince and with reports that India's killing heat made the country unworthy of conquest.

Soon after the battle of the Indus, Genghis Khan left the conquered lands in charge of his best general and went home for a brief rest. It was indeed brief. Just a year after returning to the Gobi he was on the march again, this time to subdue the Hai, a troublesome tribe in the foothills of Tibet. Then he marched against the Sung, who had continued to threaten China's southern frontier. This was his last campaign.

He had long been aware that illness was taking his strength, and when he was finally forced to remain in his tent, he sent for one of his sons. He gave instructions on continuing the campaign against the Sung and he told how his empire should be ruled.

He decreed that his oldest son, Ogotai, would be master while other sons would be governors under him, ruling various territories. A few hours after giving these orders, the great khan died. The year was 1227. Genghis Khan had lived sixty years.

Two years of mourning followed his death. His sons took up the business of empire, and they held it together. Ogotai, though not a military genius or as wise as his father, held the loyalty of the Mongols.

Fighting continued. There was a new, fierce wave of Mongol expansion that began in 1235. It led all the way to the outskirts of Vienna and the shores of the Adriatic Sea. Meanwhile, other Mongol armies took Korea and expanded their domain in China.

This expansion ended with the death of Ogotai in 1241. Rule eventually went to Kublai Khan, a grandson of Genghis. Kublai brought the Mongols their "Golden Age" from 1259 to his death in 1294. Then the empire began to break up.

Some Mongols had become Mohammedans. Others had converted to Buddhism. The Yassa lost its unifying power. Those who had once fled from the Mongols learned to fight as they did.

Tamerlane, a powerful Turkish chieftain, drove the Mongols' "Golden Horde" from the Russian Steppes. This, as we shall see, opened the door for one of history's last great migrations.

But as Genghis Khan's empire crumbled, the world was coming to terms with his legacy.

He had left Islam in such ruins that it could no longer block trade between western Europe and the Far East. Islamic princes could no longer even fight each other. Thus, there was peace at last.

Towns and cities were gradually rebuilt. Commerce, science, and the arts began to flourish. There was a freer exchange of ideas between peoples who had once been enemies. New hopes and new attitudes stimulated Europe and led to the great surge of creative energy that is known today as the Renaissance.

Was Genghis Khan responsible for the Renaissance? Hardly. But without the sweeping changes in the balance of power that his armies brought, it can be said that the timetable might have been changed. The Renaissance might have been delayed by several generations.

Without Genghis Khan, Western history certainly would have taken a different course. Life today might be a great deal different. Who knows?

Chapter Twelve

Into Siberia

The Viking expeditions and the Mongol conquest were preludes to the story of Russia's great eastward expansion. It's a strange story, and much of it is hard to believe. It still seems incredible that a small town run by tradesmen could become the seat of empire controlling a third of the Eurasian Continent. But that is exactly what happened. And it's fair to say that it happened by accident.

In prehistoric times, Russia was populated by Slavs who originated in the low country west of the Dnieper River. Some Slavs moved westward into Poland and Lithuania. Others who moved east settled in small villages along the rivers to farm, hunt, and develop river trade.

In the beginning, Moscow was an insignificant town on the Moskva River, which was also, at the time, insignificant. The people hunted in the nearby woods for fox, otter, squirrel, and beaver. The hunters used the furs of these animals to barter with the Vikings and other rivermen who occasionally ventured up the Moskva on their flat boats and cargo rafts.

When the Mongols came, Moscow was so unimportant that it was at first virtually ignored by the raiders.

The Mongols of the Russian plains, also known as Tatars, were led by Batu Khan, grandson of Genghis Khan. Batu Khan had inherited Europe as his own realm for conquest and plunder.

His campaign began in the year 1235 with a mere handful of Mongol tribesmen, just four thousand, but Batu Khan very nearly achieved his goal. After enlisting and training local nomads, including many Turks, he began a brilliant and ruthless campaign of conquest. By 1242, with Russia and Poland in his domain, he led his well disciplined cavalry into Germany. Had he not been recalled to Karakorum in that year to participate in the election of a new grand khan, he might well have conquered all of Europe.

As it was, the Tatar dominion over Russia was to last almost two centuries.

The Tatars established three zones of conquest. The home zone lay east of the Volga. There, where the great Volga swung west, closest to the Don River, they built Sarai, a magnificent capital.

In the next zone, between the Volga and the Dnieper River, the Tatars demanded submission and tribute. They also took all young men for service in the Tatar army. Few returned. If the people failed to pay tribute or meet any other Tatar demands, the penalty was slavery.

The third Tatar zone, the war zone, lay west of the Dnieper. Here the Tatar raiders were free to plunder, destroy, rape, and slaughter. Their victims, the Poles, Lithuanians, and Germans, received the brunt of the Tatar terror, but they hardened under adversity and eventually learned to oppose the Tatars and drive the bulk of their forces back to the Dnieper. Long after Batu Kahn's death in 1255, Tatar raids into the war zone continued, but the threat of European conquest was over.

The Russians, however, remained under the Tatar yoke. The Magyars and the Vikings had conditioned many of these Slavic people to subjugation.

The Magyars were nomadic horsemen who fought like the Huns. Although they originated in the Ural Mountains, they were living in the northern Caucasus region when they began their march of aggression across Russia and into the Balkans late in the ninth century. They eventually settled in what is now Hungary, but not before most slavic peasants learned to respect mounted warriors.

The Norsemen, as we have seen, came by way of the great rivers and soon controlled all river trade from the Baltic to the Black and Caspian Seas. The Dnieper, Don, and Volga Rivers, relatively secure against horse soldiers, would eventually carry goods from far-off India, and China as well as the nearer Byzantine Empire.

Greek-speaking missionaries from Byzantium also traveled up the rivers, bringing the new faith. Thus, while their Polish and Lithuanian cousins became Roman Catholics, the Russian Slavs were converted to the Greek Orthodox faith. The division has influenced history ever since.

The Vikings and Slavs interbred, and their mixed-blooded descendants remained in control of Russia until the arrival of Batu Khan and his horsemen in 1235 A.D. The invading army of Tatars, Turks, and other nomadic tribes soon became known as the Golden Horde. This was probably because of the light tan color of their tents which appeared golden in the rising sun.

Moscow, a cluster of wooden buildings on a wooded knoll above the Moskva, had no defense to speak of, but it also had very little worth taking. The Tatars were more interested in large cities such as Kiev far to the south or Vladimir, a close neighbor to Moscow. The raiders attacked these cities, took their wealth, and then demanded regular tribute from their citizens. From Moscow, Batu Kahn simply asked tribute.

Moscow did have one asset. Its location. The town stood at the southern limit of the great forest. North of Moscow it was difficult for Tatar cavalry to operate with

A statue of the legendary Rurik, the Viking who began a dynasty, now stands in Novgorod's Kremlin Square, a reminder of Russia's beginnings as a Norse trading dominion.

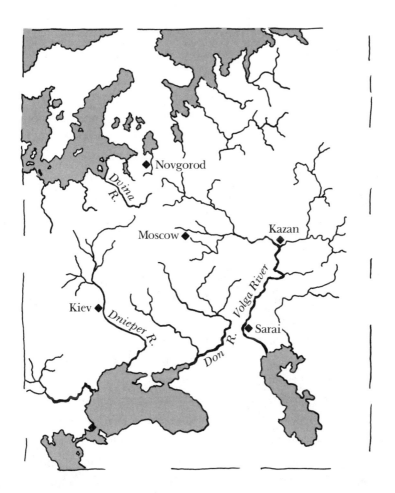

Moscow's greatest asset was its location with easy access to the headwaters of the Dvina, Dnieper, Don, and Volga Rivers.

their usual lethal efficiency. And it was easy for armed bands to ambush the horsemen. Although Novgorod, the key trade center north of Moscow, paid tribute to the Tatars, the forests saved it from armed attack.

Another important geographical asset for Moscow was the east-flowing Moskva River. Though small, it was part of the headwater system of the mighty Volga which flowed to the Caspian Sea. And a few miles to the west, by carrying their goods and their boats overland, boatmen could reach the headwaters of two other major trade routes—the Dvina River which flowed north into the Baltic, and

the Dnieper which flowed south past Kiev and on to the
Black Sea.

Thus Moscow stood at the crossroads, actually, "cross-
rivers" of trade. It was a junction that linked three seas.
The Caspian trade was fed by the caravan routes to China
and India. The Baltic led to the ports of northern Europe,
and the Black Sea led to the Mediterranean world.

Citizens of early Moscow had no concept of the town's
potential. They used their animal skins to barter with the
passing rivermen for salt, tallow, weapons, and other necessities. Many inns catered to the rivermen. When the river
froze, the boats gave way to horse-drawn sleds that followed
the river routes. Thus the fur suppliers and the innkeepers
did a brisk business all year long.

To make Moscow a more desired stopping place for
the traders, the citizens built a stockade around the town.
This gave some security against small bands of raiding
Tatars, robbers, and river pirates. The added security
combined with Moscow's insignificance attracted refugees.
Noble families, descendants of Vikings who had lost their
holdings in Kiev, Vladimir, and other cities attacked by
the Tatars, moved their families to Moscow. Thus the
small town acquired a court of nobles. The noble class
was to become the Boyars of Moscow. Their power in
governing the destiny of the country varied according to
the strength and whims of the ruling prince, who was
usually picked from the wealthiest family of merchants.

An inner fortress or Kremlin was eventually built
within the city to house the prince and his court. This
fortified compound expanded through the years to em-
brace churches, schools, stables, and other royal necessities.

The Tatar invasion drove another group of refugees
to the town on the Moskva—the churchmen. Priests and

bishops had not only lost their congregations, but they had also lost their contact with Constantinople, long the "shrine city" for the Greek Orthodox faith. A new religious center was needed. As important churchmen gathered there, Moscow began to fill the need. Far and near, the faithful looked to Moscow for leadership. The town's churches were soon boasting important religious relics. Russian peasants began to speak of "Holy Mother Moscow."

With no army and only a flimsy wooden stockade for defense, the early princes of Moscow relied on their wits for survival. They developed a keen political sense, and they knew how to be humble when necessary. Whenever a Tatar emissary or tax collector arrived outside the city, the prince went out to welcome the visitor, kiss his stirrups, and lead his horse through the city gate. Moscow paid whatever the Tatars asked and always filled the quota of young men demanded for the khan's army.

Like other towns and cities in the zone of subjugation, Moscow sent representatives to Sarai, the Tatars's rich capital city. These representatives were actually hostages, but they were generally well treated and given freedom of the city and the court. The Muscovites were usually keen observers. They studied Tsar Batu and his heirs and learned how the Tatars used their power. The men from Moscow also met fellow hostages from Russia, and because Sarai was a trade center, they met merchants from many other parts of the world.

When hostages returned to Moscow they carried with them a great deal of practical and stimulating wisdom. This probably helped spark an aggressive policy of expansion among Moscow's leading families. They became land hungry. By constantly buying land, Muscovite leaders extended their rule. The land added to the Moscow sphere was cleared and brought into production. The Tatars encouraged this expansion policy because higher production meant more tribute. Also, a farming economy tied peasants to the land, forcing them to live in small, scattered communities, lessening the chance of organized resistance.

The town's religious community, crowded with refugees, also caught the expansion fever. Missionaries were eager to go forth and establish churches and monasteries, but there was only one direction to go—northeast, into the forest and beyond the reach of the Tatars.

Fur trappers, following a convenient web of rivers, had already pioneered this region, but it was still sparsely settled when the missionaries came. But their churches and monasteries, usually well fortified, encouraged more settlement. And so the first great wave of expansion began.

Through the years, the expansion was encouraged by several other things.

The princes of Moscow ruled their domain in the manner of the Tatars. Their rule was harsh and absolute. They were greedy. The city held monopolies on the making of both alcoholic spirits and weapons. And those within the ever-expanding authority of Moscow paid heavy taxes on everything from animal pelts to farm produce. The harshest burden, however, was the need to give up young men for service in the khan's forces. By enforcing the Tatar draft, Moscow allied itself with the enemy.

For a people who treasured independence and freedom, the only escape was to the northeast, where Moscow's authority had not yet reached.

Even when the Tatars began to lose their grip over subjugated lands, Moscow continued to rule in the Tatar manner. Although the Moskovy princes stopped paying Tatar tribute, they continued to collect taxes. The town grew rich, and its wealth attracted attention.

In 1380, a Lithuanian army crossed the Dnieper into Russia with plans to join forces with the remnants of a Tatar army and then march on Moscow. The Tatars demanded renewal of tribute. Dmitri, the leading Moskovy prince of the day, refused and did something unheard of in the history of the city. He mobilized an army.

What the new army lacked in training and leadership it made up for in zeal. The Muscovites attacked the Tatars before the Lithuanians could join them. It was a bloody battle, but the Tatars fled. The Russian people were electrified by the victory. It planted the seed of national pride.

Two years later, however, the Tatars took revenge. They attacked Moscow, forced the city gates, looted the city, and then put it to the torch. Dmitri, who had fled the enemy, returned to the ruins where some twenty-four thousand Muscovites lay dead. Dmitri reportedly paid for the burials from his own purse. And payment of Tatar tribute from the state treasury was resumed.

As the fourteenth century drew to a close, however, the vast Mongol empire began to crumble. In the east, the Mongols were driven out of China. In the west, Tamerlane organized several nomadic bands into a powerful force that was to drive the Golden Horde from the Russian plains. Tamerlane eventually built an empire that embraced Syria, Persia, Southern Russia, and part of India, but when he died, his domain, divided among his heirs, quickly lost its standing as a world force.

In Russia, the Tatars retained a few centers of power. The Volga Tatars, with their fortified capitol at Kazan, four hundred miles east of Moscow, controlled trade on the mighty river. The Crimean or Krim Tatars occupied the north shores of the Black Sea, where they controlled trade down the Don and Dnieper Rivers. When Moscow traders were allowed to use these rivers it was at the expense of heavy Tatar tariff.

Access to the Baltic ports was controlled by Novgorod, the ancient trade center northwest of Moscow. The merchants of Novgorod had long-standing trade agreements with German and Swedish merchants. Poles and Lithuanians also benefited from the trade. In fact, Novgorod had become an international city with a large population of cultured, well-educated merchants. For almost all Baltic trade, Moscow merchants had to deal with the haughty Novgorod traders.

Moscow, meanwhile, was gaining an abundance of goods. It needed foreign markets desperately.

Dmitri ruled in the Kremlin until his death in 1505. He was followed by Vasily III who expanded Moscow's authority, but failed to solve the trade problem. After Vasily's death in 1533, Moscow was ruled indecisively by various Boyar factions. Ivan, the young heir to the throne, escaped assassination only because the Boyars could not agree on a successor. At the age of sixteen, after teaching himself to read and write, Ivan took the reins of government in a firm grip.

Generally known today as Ivan the Terrible, Ivan IV was one of history's more complex characters. Always cruel to his enemies, late in his reign he went so far as to organize a secret society of terrorists, which he often led in night raids against the Boyar families who opposed him. Many nobles were slaughtered and their property confiscated. Some Boyars were exiled. Others fled out of fear. Most went east. For Ivan, the raids won the love of the

Ivan IV, 1530–1584.

peasants and merchant class who had suffered under Boyar
rule.

Ivan matched an ungoverned temper with an endless
curiosity. He demanded absolute loyalty, yet he was suspicious of all those about him. He admired foreigners for
their wit and knowledge and envied and mistrusted them
for the same reasons. He was generous to the church and
the poor, but he was just as greedy about levying taxes and
acquiring property as his predecessors.

Among the common people, he encouraged self-
government, yet he was the first prince of Moscow to call
himself tsar, or emperor.

Ivan set out to solve the trade problem by attacking
the Volga Tatar stronghold at Kazan. It was a long, difficult campaign. The Tatars fought bravely, but they had
no defense against the Muscovite siege guns. When the

fortress fell in 1555, the way eastward opened. New wealth began flowing into Moscow, but access to the Baltic remained in the hands of Novgorod merchants.

A long war for control of the Baltic began. The Muscovites won some early victories against the Poles and the Swedes, but then the fighting bogged down into long, indecisive, and costly campaigns. The unpopular war dragged on for twenty-four years. Novgorod, forced into an uneasy alliance with the tsar, was doomed. In 1570, suspecting a Novgorod plot against him, Ivan sent a ravaging army into the city. He executed some leaders and relocated others, sending them and their families to live in distant territories. This relocation policy continued into our own era as a Russian "solution" for dissent.

Meanwhile, voluntary relocation was in full stream from other areas under Moscow's rule. To escape heavy war taxes and service in the tsar's unpopular war, the more vigorous and ambitious of the Russian people followed the missionaries into the northeast. The roads and the rivers led all the way to the White Sea above the Arctic Circle. Here, under Ivan's encouragement, English traders had begun to arrive. They paid handsomely for Russian furs. With the pelt of one fox, a trapper could earn enough from the English to retire for the rest of his life. Stories of such easy wealth started a land rush.

The new thrust of migration pressured the trappers and farmers who were already settled in the northeast. They picked up roots and moved south into the area that had been opened by the defeat of the Volga Tatars. Many of the new migrants, after finding the northeast climate too cold and the growing season too short, also turned south, joining others who were beginning to move due east from Moscow.

Ivan could do nothing to control this migration. He did, however, make huge grants of land beyond the Volga to some of his favored Boyars. The Stroganov family thus gained an empire that could be ruled with little interference from Moscow. This distant empire bordered the Kama River and extended all the way to the Ural Mountains.

Beyond making land grants, Ivan paid little attention to the Eastern frontier. He continued to struggle for the Baltic. Southern territories were also left to their own destiny.

Tatars and Turks controlled much of the vast and rich Russian Steppes in the Dnieper, Don, and Volga River basins, but their control was now challenged by brotherhoods of roaming bands who became known as Cossacks. The word apparently came from the Turkish *kozak*, meaning masterful husband.

The Cossacks ruled much like the Tatars; in fact, some were Tatar renegades. Many had Tatar blood. Others were Slavs who had served the Tatars for many years before escaping into the vast steppe. Escaped criminals and slaves also joined Cossack bands. These fierce men, who put little value on life, treasured freedom and wealth. They demanded tribute from farmers and merchants. Sometimes, if the pay was good, they served in Ivan's army. Eventually, they were to become the backbone of Russia's military might.

Usually, however, the early Cossacks opposed Moscow. It represented taxation, fines, regulations, laws, and loss of freedom. A Cossack was loyal to the leader of his band —no one else.

Yermak Timofeivitch was such a leader. He was born on the Kama River east of Kazan, the bastard son of a

Danish slave woman. He grew to be a bearded, blue-eyed giant who at age twenty-one was condemned to death for stealing horses. He escaped to the Volga where he organized a band of river pirates. When Ivan sent armed patrols to catch the thieving Cossacks, Yermak led his band, now numbering more than five hundred, back to the Kama. There they made a compact with the Stroganovs. The Cossacks, in exchange for Stroganov weapons and shelter, would not steal Stroganov livestock. Instead they would patrol the huge domain and keep it free of squatters, fur poachers, and Tatar raiders.

Although the Cossacks kept their agreement with the Stroganovs, Yermak and his men frequently raided neighboring lands. Ivan, nearing the end of his long reign, was outraged. He sent an armed force with orders to arrest the Cossacks.

Upon learning of the tsar's anger, Yermak led his band, which now numbered more than eight hundred, eastward. The tough Cossacks hauled their boats through a pass in the Ural Mountains. They came to a small river where they launched their craft and slowly continued eastward. They had entered an unmapped wilderness that had long been ruled by the Tatars. There Yermak sought the legendary Tatar fortress of Sibir, the landmark that was to give Siberia its name.

Winter came. The river froze. The Cossacks built log cabins and waited for spring. Many passed the time hunting sable and beaver. The land was rich in fur. When the river flowed again, Yermak led his band onward. Tatar bands followed along the bank, raining arrows on the boats whenever the river narrowed. Tatars also attacked Cossack foragers.

Because Cossack firearms were superior to the Tatar

bows, Yermak knew he could hold a defended position, but his bands of hunters and trappers were vulnerable. Yermak would not let his men stray far from the river. Just the same, some were killed or wounded by Tatar arrows.

Yermak fortified a knoll at the junction of the Upper Ob and Irtish Rivers. From there, he sent a band against a nearby Tatar camp. Captives from the raid revealed that Sibir was just a few miles away. Yermak led all his men against it. They found it abandoned. The main body of Tatars had retreated to the south.

Yermak demanded tribute from the surrounding tribes. The placid natives, who had long been paying tribute to the Tatars, did not object. Meanwhile, the Cossacks gathered a treasure in furs.

Deciding to spend the winter of 1583–84 at Sibir, Yermak sent a trusted lieutenant to Moscow with a gift intended to placate the tsar. Figures were probably exaggerated, but the peace offering was said to include the skins of 1,592 sables, 6,182 ermine, 192 white fox, 610 bears, assorted rubies and diamonds, and several pounds of silver and gold.

No matter what the actual numbers were, Yermak's gift was large enough to catch Ivan's attention. The dynamic leader who had spent most of his energies trying to expand and consolidate his western empire, at last turned his attention to the east. Perhaps he finally realized that Russia's destiny lay in Siberia.

The tsar forgot Yermak's crimes and sent gifts, including a breastplate bearing the double eagles of Moscow, to the Cossack. He also sent a regular army detachment to garrison Sibir, and he granted a vast new realm beyond the Urals to the Stroganovs.

What Ivan might have done further, we can only guess. He died in 1584, leaving only a feeble-minded son as heir to the throne. Another son, who had been destined to rule, was killed earlier when Ivan, in a fit of rage, struck the boy with his scepter.

Ruling as regent for the feeble-minded boy, Boris Godunov, a court advisor who had long advocated eastern expansion, encouraged settlement beyond the Urals. But the government, no matter what its policies, actually had little influence on coming events.

Certainly, the government could not save Yermak. Tatar horsemen, returning from the south, caught and almost eliminated one Cossack party that had gone out in search of the Muscovite soldiers promised by the tsar. And when the soldiers finally did arrive, they were exhausted from travel and from fighting Tatars. The men had abandoned most of the gunpowder and other provisions that Yermak desperately needed.

Nevertheless, he held the Sibir garrison together for another winter. When spring came he went in search of a caravan reportedly carrying food and gunpowder. He never found it. Instead, while camped on a riverbank, his scouting party was overwhelmed by Tatars. Yermak jumped in the water and tried to swim to a boat. But he sank out of sight, weighed down by the breastplate bearing the double eagles.

Legends of Yermak and his men have been told ever since. According to some accounts, Yermak explored all of Siberia. This, of course, was an exaggeration. He simply opened the gates. They turned out to be floodgates.

By the time of Yermak's death, the region around the Upper Volga and the Kama had become crowded with restless people. Many of them were second generation pioneers, having grown up in the northeast territory and then moved south following the defeat of the Volga Tatars. Others were Cossacks, many of whom had been driven from the Steppes by Polish invaders. All were accustomed to hardship, were distrustful of government officials, and were eager to explore new lands.

Tales of Yermak's rich discovery were all these people needed. The tales of fortunes to be won in furs were to Siberia what the tales of California gold were to the American West, except the furs were more plentiful and more easily had than the elusive gold.

Siberia was sparsely populated by primitive hunters little advanced from the stone age. Although they were not above murdering a lone trapper, the concept of warfare was completely alien to them. They were also innocent of commerce. Advance parties of trappers often traded a bottle of vodka or a handful of beads for a fortune in native pelts. Many trappers did not even bother with the formality of barter. They simply took the native pelts, enslaved the native women, and then demanded tribute.

The natives, who had experienced the same treatment from the Tatars, made little protest. They were outraged, however, when the hunters killed reindeer, bear, or other game instead of waiting for these animals to die naturally. Under native belief, the offended spirits of these animals would haunt the hunters to an early grave.

The Russian pioneers bred freely with the native women so that, after a few generations, pure-blooded natives were a rarity. But because they did not resist, the native Siberians often fared better in the face of conquest than the American Indian. Though reduced, the Samoyede, Tungus, Chukchi, Kamchatkan, Koryak, and many other primitive cultures still exist in modern Siberia.

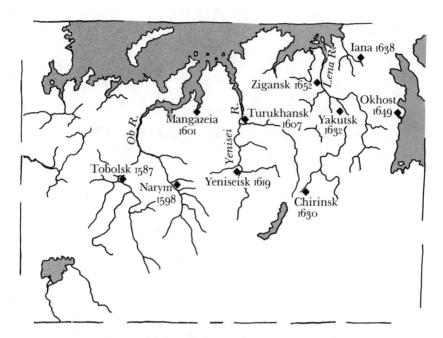

*The establishment of government forts, usually a decade or so
behind the arrival of the first settlers, shows the rapid progress
of Siberian expansion.*

The first wave of pioneers was followed by a collection of foreign adventurers—Poles, Germans, Lithuanians, Swedes, and many others. Then came government agents to collect taxes, to make sure native tribute was collected and sent to the tsar, and to manage land grants. Many government agents grew rich by skimming off their own cut of taxes and tribute they collected. The free-spirited trappers moved farther east whenever government agents appeared.

But the government did build forts and garrison them with troops, providing enough security for colonists to farm, harvest timber, and dig for ore. The Tatars were still a strong enough threat to force the tide of migration to veer northward, away from the Tatar strength. The tsar's agents visited Karakorum and demanded tribute from the minor Mongol chief who was in charge there.

He refused them. So did the emperor of China. These rebuffs, however, did not dampen the Russian zeal for conquest.

The list of government forts reveals the speed of that conquest. It all happened in a generation. Tobolsk was built on the west fork of the Ob in 1587. Narym was built on the east fork in 1598. Far to the north, Mangazeia was built on the Gulf of the Ob in 1601.

Turukhansk halfway up the Yenisei River was built in 1607. Fort Yeniseisk further south went up in 1619. Chirinsk at the headwaters of the Lena River, was built in 1630. Other Lena forts, Zigansk and Yakutsk were built in 1632. Farther east, Iana was built in 1638 and Okhost on the shores of the Pacific Ocean in 1649.

Russia's eastward expansion stopped only briefly. In 1741, Tsar Peter I sent the Danish explorer Vitus Bering across the sea that now bears his name to the coast of Alaska. Russia claimed the huge peninsula and went on to establish fur trading outposts down the shores of the Pacific Northwest into Northern California.

Fort Ross, the vanguard of these outposts, continued in operation until 1841 when the Russians moved out, selling the guns, rifles, powder, and other gear to a Swiss by the name of John Sutter who was equipping his own fort on the Sacramento River. Sutter's Fort was to play a key role in the winning of the American West.

The wave of migration had come full circle.

B I B L I O G R A P H Y

BULFINCH, THOMAS. *Bulfinch's Mythology*. New York: Random House, 1947.

DURANT, WILL. *The Age of Faith*. New York: Simon and Schuster, 1950.

———. *Caesar and Christ*. New York: Simon and Schuster, 1944.

———. *Our Oriental Heritage*. New York: Simon and Schuster, 1954.

FRAZER, SIR JAMES GEORGE. *The Golden Bough*. New York: The Macmillan Company, 1955.

GORDON, CYRUS H. *The Ancient Near East*. New York: The Norton Library, 1965.

GREENFIELD, HOWARD. *Gypsies*. New York: Crown Publishers, 1977.

HADAS, MOSES, and the editors of Time-Life Books. *Imperial Rome*. New York: Time-Life Books, 1965.

HASKINS, CHARLES HOMER. *The Normans in European History*. New York: W. W. Norton & Company, 1943.

KOHN, BERNICE. *The Gypsies*. New York: Bobbs-Merrill, 1972.

LAMB, HAROLD. *The March of the Muscovy*. Garden City, NY: Doubleday & Company, 1948.

———. *Genghis Khan, Emperor of All Men*. New York: Robert M. McBride, & Company, 1927.

———. *Tamerlane, the Earth Shaker*. Garden City, NY: Garden City Publishing Company, 1928.

————. *Theodora and the Emperor*. New York: Bantam Books, 1952.

LATHAM, RONALD, translator. *The Travels of Marco Polo*. Baltimore, MD: Penguin Books, 1967.

MAGNUSSON, MAGNUS. *Viking Expansion Westwards*. New York: Henry Z. Walck, Inc., 1973.

McDOWELL, BART. *Gypsies, Wanderers of the World*. Washington, DC: National Geographic Society, 1970.

MAENCHEN-HELFEN, OTTO J. *The World of the Huns: Studies in their History and Culture*. Berkeley, CA: University of California Press, 1973.

MENON, B. P. "Gypsies Who Never Left Home," New York: *GEO*, May, 1983.

SIMONS, GERALD, and editors of Time-Life Books. *Barbarian Europe*. New York: Time-Life Books, 1968.

TIME-LIFE BOOKS, editors. *The Epic of Man*. New York: Time-Life Books, 1961.

WARNER, REX, translator. *War Commentaries of Caesar*. New York: New American Library, 1963.

WILSON, D. M. *The Anglo-Saxons*. New York: Frederick A. Praeger, 1962.

YOORS, JAN. *The Gypsies*. New York: Simon and Schuster, 1969.

I N D E X